W9-CPH-239

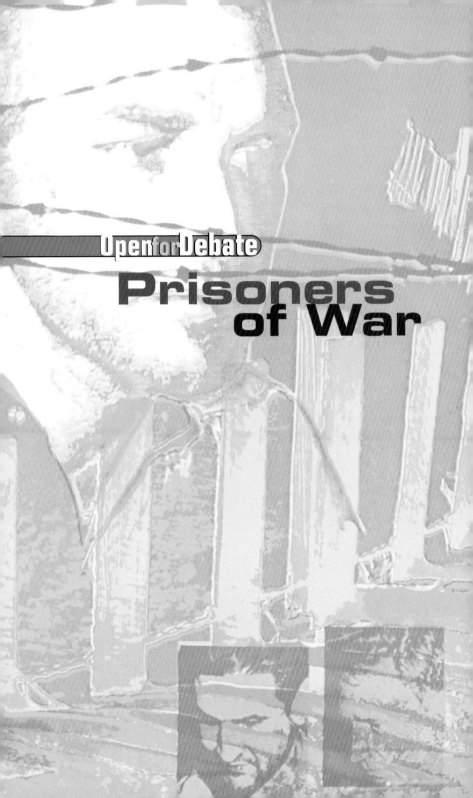

Open for Debate

Prisoners of War

Open for Debate

Prisoners
of War

Ron Fridell

mc **Marshall Cavendish**
Benchmark
New York

42.95

Marshall Cavendish Benchmark
99 White Plains Road
Tarrytown, NY 10591
www.marshallcavendish.us
Copyright © 2008 by Marshall Cavendish Corporation

All Internet sites were available and accurate when sent to press.

Library of Congress Cataloging-in-Publication Data
Fridell, Ron.
Prisoners of war / by Ron Fridell.
p. cm.—(Open for debate)
Summary: "Discusses the debate over treatment and rights of prisoners of
war, including an historical discussion of POWs"—Provided by publisher.
Includes bibliographical references and index.
ISBN-13: 978-0-7614-2577-9
1. Prisoners of war—Legal status, laws, etc.—Juvenile literature. 2.
Prisoners of war—United States.—History—Juvenile literature. I. Title.
II. Series.
KZ6495.F75 2007
341.6'5—dc22 2006030371

Photo research by Lindsay Aveilhe and Linda Sykes/
Linda Sykes Picture Research, Inc., Hilton Head, SC

Time Magazine/Time & Life Pictures/Getty Images: cover, 6;
Getty Images: 10; CORBIS: 17, 60; Bettmann/CORBIS: 23, 31, 57, 63, 73;
Imagno/Getty Images: 26; Getty Images: 32; Library of Congress: 40; Topham Picturepoint/
The Image Works: 47; dpa/Corbis: 48; The Granger Collection: 52; Jacques Langevin/
Corbis Sygma: 76; FBI Handout/CNP/Corbis: 82; AP/Wide World Photos: 86;
Handout/Reuters/Corbis: 99; The Washington Post/Corbis: 106;
AP/Wide World Photos: 118, 122; Art Levin/Pool/Reuters/Corbis: 131

Publisher: Michelle Bisson
Art Director: Anahid Hamparian
Series Designer: Sonia Chaghatzbanian

Printed in China

1 3 5 6 4 2

Contents

FIFTY CENTS

TIME

The Plight of the Prisoners

Introduction

The Navy pilot had just taken off from an aircraft carrier. His attack plane was on its way to bomb a power plant in North Vietnam. The date was October 26, 1967. This would be his twenty-third mission as a fighter pilot in the Vietnam War (1965–1973). It would also be his last. The pilot was rolling the plane into a dive when he saw something coming at him. Then, he remembers, "[A] missile the size of a telephone pole blew the right wing off the Skyhawk bomber which I was piloting."

His aircraft had taken a direct hit from a surface-to-air missile. The plane immediately burst into flames and dropped into a downward spin. The pilot had no choice but to eject. He was shot straight out of the aircraft. When he was a safe distance away, a parachute was deployed, but he never saw it open. The force of the ejection had knocked him cold.

"I regained consciousness as I parachuted into a lake," the pilot recalled. He did not realize it yet, but he had broken his right leg at the knee and both arms in three places.

"My helmet and oxygen mask had been blown off. With my fifty pounds of equipment and gear I sank to the bottom. I rose and then started sinking. I could not understand why I could not use my right arm or leg."

He was badly shaken and confused. "The third time I sank I couldn't get back to the surface." Yet he somehow kept his wits about him. "With my teeth I was finally able to get the toggle released thus inflating the life preserver which floated me to the top."

Eventually the badly injured pilot was fished from the waters of Truc Bac, a lake in central Hanoi, and then handed over to the enemy. The pilot was U.S. Navy Lieutenant Commander John S. McCain III.

Up to that moment Lieutenant Commander McCain was a combatant in a war between nations. After that he lost combatant status and took on a new identity. He was now a POW, a prisoner of war.

1
The Issues

Prisoners of war present difficult problems for their captors. Vital people and supplies must be devoted to their care. Soldiers who could be actively fighting enemy combatants must now spend their time guarding prisoners. Medical personnel needed to tend to their own side's sick and wounded must also treat the enemy. Vital food and clothing needed by friendly soldiers in the field must go to enemy captives instead.

In wartime, people and materials are often in short supply. How much care should these prisoners receive? Or should they get any care at all? To what rights, if any, are these prisoners entitled? After all, this is war, and prisoners are the enemy. Why not simply execute captives on the spot and move on?

Who Are They?

These and other perplexing questions have been posed during wars all through human history, including the War

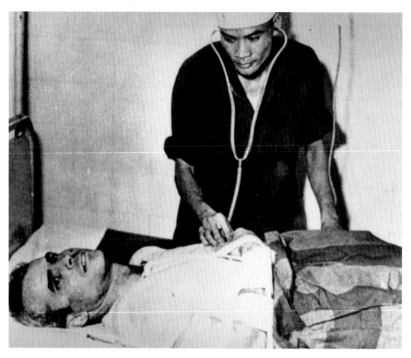

JOHN MCCAIN WAS A PRISONER OF WAR IN A HANOI HOSPITAL IN 1967. NORTH VIETNAMESE DOCTORS NEVER PROPERLY SET HIS BROKEN LIMBS. AS A RESULT, MCCAIN WAS NEVER AGAIN ABLE TO LIFT HIS ARMS ABOVE HIS SHOULDERS.

on Terrorism. Each question represents an issue to be discussed and debated, beginning with the most basic question of all: Exactly how should a prisoner of war be defined and regarded?

Are POWs restricted to conventional soldiers captured on the field of battle, wearing the uniform of a rival nation at war? Or may they also be captured members of unconventional fighting forces, such as rebel armies or militias? What about terrorists? Should combatants captured by U.S. fighting forces in the War on Terrorism, such as members of the Taliban, a fundamentalist Islamic militia from Afghanistan, or Al-Qaeda, a worldwide network of Islamic terrorists, be considered prisoners of war and treated as such?

Before nations can decide how to treat POWs, they must settle on a point of view. How should prisoners of war be regarded? Should they be seen as enemy combatants who must be harshly confined and punished until the war's end? Should they be regarded as slaves to be used for forced labor, even after the war is over; or as kidnap victims to be held for ransom; or as helpless villains to be mocked and reviled? Or should they be viewed not as enemies but as ordinary soldiers who are no longer combatants and who must be treated with respect and compassion until the war's end?

At one time or another, prisoners of war have been viewed in all these varied ways. Which of these points of view are appropriate? How should prisoners of war be defined, regarded, and treated in today's world?

What Are Their Rights?

If we assume that prisoners of war should be granted certain rights, what should those rights be? Are POWs entitled to the same basic shelter, nourishment, clothing, and medical care that the soldiers of the captor nation receive? Or should they be given only enough of the bare necessities to remain alive?

The International Committee of the Red Cross (ICRC) is a humanitarian organization involved with the rights of prisoners of war. Should organizations such as the ICRC be allowed to inspect POW camps to check on whether prisoners are being granted their rights?

What about punishment? Should prisoners of war be free from punishment, provided they follow the basic rules of behavior set down by their captors? Or should their captors be allowed to abuse and humiliate them as they see fit?

What about interrogations? Should POWs enjoy the right to refuse to answer questions concerning their nation's military operations, such as revealing the secret locations of troops or weapons, without fear of reprisal? Or should their captors feel free to go to any lengths, including physical and psychological torture, to force prisoners to reveal military secrets?

What legal rights should POWs be granted? Suppose prisoners are accused of committing war crimes, such as deliberately targeting and killing civilians. Should those POW suspects be granted the same legal rights as civilian criminal suspects? Should they enjoy the right to be told the crime of which they are accused and to be confronted with the evidence against them? Should they have the right to be represented by legal counsel in a trial conducted in a traditional civilian or military court? If found not guilty, should they enjoy the right to be set free from confinement? Or should their captors be allowed to keep them confined forever, whether found guilty or not guilty, with no hope of ever being set free?

A National Debate

If the history of international prisoner-of-war rights could be summarized in the form of a line graph, that line would show a steady ascent, beginning in 1864. Year by year and war by war, new issues have been debated, and prisoners have been granted more and more rights in the form of agreements signed by nearly all the world's nations, including the United States.

Then came the War on Terrorism, and many of those agreed-upon rights were abruptly called into question by the commander in chief of U.S. military forces, President George W. Bush. The president and members of his

The ICRC in Action

What happens when representatives from the International Committee of the Red Cross inspect POW camps and meet with POWs? Talking with TV reporter Margaret Warner, ICRC spokesperson Amanda Williamson explains.

WILLIAMSON: First of all, it's important that we register them. . . . Then we . . . demand what we call private interviews. Every prisoner has the chance to speak privately with an ICRC delegate. Any concerns that he or she may have about their conditions and treatment we treat confidentially and raise those with the detaining authorities. And also, vitally important . . . is the value that the Red Cross message has. This is often the only lifeline that the prisoners have with their families in the outside world, and they write a Red Cross message, and we deliver that to families. It's a really vital humanitarian part of the work that we do in prison.

WARNER: Do you come out, though, and report to the world on the treatment of the prisoners?

WILLIAMSON: No, we don't. . . . [A]nything that we see . . . is treated absolutely confidentially. We share this with the detaining authorities to try to address any problems that the prisoner or we have raised. It's really vitally important for us that we gain access and continue to gain access. That's why we maintain the process.

administration insisted that captured terrorists did not qualify as prisoners of war and so did not need to be granted POW rights.

However, the president insisted, this did not mean that War on Terrorism prisoners were being abused. The Bush administration kept insisting that all prisoners were being treated humanely, even as evidence kept surfacing that many prisoners were in fact being abused, tortured, and even murdered. The administration was more forthright about legal matters. Officials insisted upon denying War on Terrorism prisoners key legal rights.

These developments led to a fiery national debate that eventually involved the U.S. Supreme Court, the executive branch, and both houses of Congress. The American public joined in the debate, either siding with or against the administration on prisoner-of-war issues. To fully appreciate these issues and the debate involved, it is first necessary to look at how prisoner-of-war rights have evolved through time.

2
POWs and the Laws of War

War, the use of violence to impose one nation's or faction's will on another, is as old as human history. What is war like for the people who take part in it? Georges Clemenceau was France's prime minister during World War I (1914–1918). "War is a series of catastrophes that results in a victory," he declared. Dwight D. Eisenhower, Supreme Commander of the Allied forces in Europe during World War II (1939–1945), said, "I hate war as only a soldier who has lived it can, only as one who has seen its brutality, its futility, its stupidity."

Catastrophic, hated, brutal, futile, stupid: not exactly a glowing picture. For the people who must fight it, war is a tragic, ugly, chaotic business.

Early Laws of War

Yet war has always had its laws and customs, even in ancient times. Some were written down. Others remained unwritten but were assumed to be understood by all.

War Is Hell

In this famous news dispatch from World War II, war correspondent Ernie Pyle describes the reality of a U.S. infantry soldier's everyday life. The place is northern Tunisia and the date is May 2, 1943.

I wish you could see just one of the ineradicable pictures I have in my mind today. In this particular picture I am sitting among clumps of sword-grass on a steep and rocky hillside that we have just taken. We are looking out over a vast rolling country to the rear.

A narrow path comes like a ribbon over a hill miles away, down a long slope, across a creek, up a slope and over another hill.

All along the length of this ribbon there is now a thin line of men. For four days and nights they have fought hard, eaten little, washed none, and slept hardly at all. Their nights have been violent with attack, fright, butchery, and their days sleepless and miserable with the crash of artillery.

The men are walking. They are fifty feet apart, for dispersal. Their walk is slow, for they are dead weary, as you can tell even when looking at them from behind. Every line and sag of their bodies speaks their inhuman exhaustion.

On their shoulders and backs they carry heavy steel tripods, machine-gun barrels, leaden boxes of ammunition. Their feet seem to sink into the ground from the overload they are bearing.

They don't slouch. It is the terrible deliberation of each step that spells out their appalling tiredness. Their faces are black and unshaven. They are young men, but the grime and whiskers and exhaustion make them look middle-aged.

In their eyes as they pass is not hatred, not excitement, not despair, not the tonic of their victory—there is just the simple expression of being here as though they had been here doing this forever, and nothing else.

The line moves on, but it never ends. All afternoon men keep coming round the hill and vanishing eventually over the horizon. It is one long tired line of antlike men.

PRIZE-WINNING CORRESPONDENT ERNIE PYLE TYPES OUT A NEWS STORY IN ANZIO, ITALY. PYLE TRAVELED WITH U.S. TROOPS DURING WORLD WAR II, PUTTING HIMSELF IN HARM'S WAY TO GET THEIR DRAMATIC STORIES. NEAR THE END OF THE WAR, PYLE WAS KILLED BY JAPANESE MACHINE-GUN FIRE.

Perhaps the oldest law of war is the one that excuses the warrior from murder. Since ancient times, a combatant who injures or kills other combatants in battle is not seen as a murderer in the legal sense of the word.

Why? Because a murderer kills for himself, while a combatant kills for a government or a cause. That's why soldiers wear uniforms: uniforms identify the soldiers as agents of their government. As long as their actions conform to the laws and customs of war, soldiers cannot be held responsible for the damage they do in combat, and that includes soldiers taken prisoner.

Here was a strong reason for arguing that prisoners of war ought to be treated with respect and compassion. But in ancient times, most armies did not accept this line of reasoning. If you were captured, you could expect to be tortured, starved, or murdered. Or you might be held for ransom or made a slave and worked to death. You might even be taken back to the battlefield and used as a human shield.

Calls for Compassion

These brutal punishments prompted calls for humane treatment of POWs from cultures around the world. In 400 BCE, in his book *The Art of War*, Chinese general Sun Tzu wrote that soldiers must treat their captives well and care for them. Dating from the first century CE, the Hindu law code of Manu states that soldiers must refrain from attacking one who "joins palms of hands, sits down, flees, or says 'I am yours.'" In other words, a soldier who surrenders.

St. Augustine, one of the fathers of the Christian church, urged soldiers never to regard the enemy as subhuman and lacking in human rights. And in the eighteenth century, French philosopher Jean-Jacques Rousseau formulated this principle of warfare:

Since the object of war is to destroy the enemy State, it is legitimate to kill the latter's defenders as long as they are carrying arms; but as soon as they lay them down and surrender, they cease to be enemies or agents of the enemy, and again become mere men, and it is no longer legitimate to take their lives.

"Treat Them with Humanity"

During the American Revolutionary War (1775–1783), George Washington and his Continental army put these laws of war into practice, even as their opponents did not. The British claimed that Washington's Colonial soldiers were not legitimate combatants in a war between nations. Instead, they were rebels illegally attempting to break away from their mother country of Great Britain. These illegal combatants were not entitled to the rights of prisoners of war. Rather than take Colonial soldiers captive, the British said, they would execute them on the battlefield.

The British made good on their threat. In one notorious incident, seven Colonial soldiers surrendered during the battle at Drake's Farm, and British troops murdered all seven by crushing their heads with their muskets.

The Americans took a different view. They believed that all captives should be taken prisoner. After winning the Battle of Trenton, on Christmas Day 1776, Washington found himself left with hundreds of troops who had fought for the British and surrendered. Washington ordered his troops to take the prisoners in and "treat them with humanity," which they did. "Let them have no reason to complain of our copying the brutal example of the British army," Washington said.

Thus, George Washington and his Colonial troops began a long tradition of humane treatment of prisoners of war in the United States. Washington's reasons, while based on compassionate morals and ethics, were concrete and practical as well. First, of course, treating POWs humanely was the right thing to do. But also, it might persuade some of these soldiers to change their allegiance and fight for the American side, which was just what happened.

Deadly Conditions

Washington's humanitarian approach helped advance the treatment of POWs. The next important advance occurred when, for the first time in history, the laws of war were organized into a formal code. That would occur nearly a century later, during the American Civil War (1861–1865).

Sometimes it takes a desperate situation to spark real change, and the treatment of Civil War prisoners was desperate indeed. One reason was race. When African Americans started showing up in uniform for the Union Army, the Confederate government issued an ominous declaration: captured black soldiers would be treated as fugitive slaves instead of prisoners of war, which might well lead to their being enslaved, tortured, or murdered.

So President Abraham Lincoln issued General Order 233. This order threatened to mistreat Confederate prisoners if the South should carry through on its threat toward black Union prisoners. It was a strong reason for treating black prisoners humanely.

Lincoln's counterthreat helped keep black prisoners alive. While white captives on both sides suffered harsh treatment themselves, especially Union soldiers taken prisoner by the South, black POWs were treated even less humanely.

The Confederate government was constantly short of funds. It could barely supply the basic needs of its combat troops, let alone captured Yankees. Here was an obvious reason for not treating prisoners of war humanely. How could they be given adequate shelter, food, and clothing, when these materials were not available to be given?

The harsh conditions at some Southern POW camps led to suffering and death. The camp at Andersonville, Georgia, was particularly notorious. More than 45,000 Union soldiers were sent there; nearly 13,000 died from disease, malnutrition, or exposure.

The Lieber Code

Besides the harsh conditions in POW camps, other problems stemmed from the loose manner in which Confederate troops were sometimes organized. Some men who did not have uniforms formed small groups to defend their homes against the invading Yankees. How were these irregular, nonuniformed combatants to be treated?

No one was quite sure. The laws were not clear. So President Lincoln turned to Francis Lieber, a university professor, legal scholar, and former soldier, for help. Lincoln asked him to write a training manual for Union soldiers that would present the laws and customs of war in plain and simple terms.

Lieber turned out to be the right man for the job. When it came to war, he was of two attitudes: tough-minded on the one hand and humane on the other. His manual, the "Lieber Code," contained a section on the proper treatment of prisoners of war. Notice how the third passage addresses Lincoln's General Order 233.

> • **Military necessity does not admit of cruelty— that is, the infliction of suffering for the sake of suffering or for revenge, nor of maiming or wounding except in fight, nor of torture to extort confessions.**

Life at Andersonville

Many of the Union prisoners in the Andersonville POW camp, in southwestern Georgia, were on their own when it came to shelter. There is an old saying: Necessity is the mother of invention. The necessity for shelter brought out these men's inventive natures.

The ingenious do-it-yourself "homes" they constructed were known as shebangs. Mud bricks, cloth, tree limbs, brush, almost anything they could scrounge went into these shelters. One group of prisoners actually sewed their shebang. They stitched together clothing, including shirt sleeves, along with coffee and sugar sacks. Their shebang even included a flap from a prisoner's knapsack.

Naturally, the harsh conditions made prisoners want to escape. Again, necessity was the mother of invention. Here is one of the more ingenious methods, described in the 1864 diary of Andersonville prisoner John McElroy: "A funny way of escape has just been discovered. . . . A man pretends to be dead and is carried on a stretcher, left with the row of the dead. As soon as it gets dark Mr. Deadman jumps up and runs."

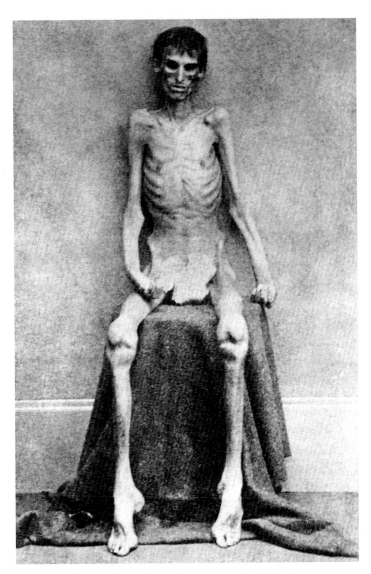

THIS CIVIL WAR PRISONER BEARS STARK WITNESS TO THE FACT THAT UNION CAPTIVES WERE DYING OF STARVATION IN CONFEDERATE CAMPS. HE IS SHOWN UPON HIS RELEASE FROM CAMP SUMTER IN ANDERSONVILLE, GEORGIA.

• **A prisoner of war is subject to no punishment for being a public enemy, nor is any revenge wreaked upon him by the intentional infliction of any suffering, or disgrace, by cruel imprisonment, want of food, by mutilation, death, or any other barbarity.**

• **The law of nations knows of no distinction of color, and if an enemy of the United States should enslave and sell any captured persons of their Army, it would be a case for the severest retaliation, if not redressed upon complaint. The United States cannot retaliate by enslavement; therefore death must be the retaliation for this crime against the law of nations.**

• **It is against the usage of modern war to . . . give no quarter [take no prisoners, but kill them instead]. . . . [B]ut a commander is permitted to direct his troops to give no quarter, in great straits, when his own salvation makes it impossible to cumber himself with [be responsible for] prisoners.**

The Lieber Code marked the first time that the laws and customs of war had been formally gathered together into a comprehensive code. The code had its limitations, though. It mentioned "the law of nations," but it was intended only for the Union soldiers fighting in the Civil War. Someone needed to do what Lieber had done on an international basis, so that all nations could refer to one common code of laws and customs of war.

3
Humanitarian Ideals

The village of Castiglione is in the north of Italy. A bloody battle was fought at the nearby town of Solferino in 1859, as part of the Second War of Italian Unification. On the evening of the battle, a Swiss businessman arrived in Castiglione. His name was Henri Dunant. What Dunant saw there moved him deeply. He saw wounded victims from both of the clashing armies. More than 9,000 of them had taken refuge in the little town, but no one had come to care for them.

Two Questions

The sight inspired more than mere compassion in Dunant. He felt the need to do something actively for these distressed people. So he hurried through the town rousing everyone he could find to lend a hand.

The citizens of Castiglione helped Dunant set up a makeshift hospital in the main church. For several days and nights, victims of combat from both sides came there

THIS PAINTING DEPICTS THE BATTLE OF SOLFERINO, 1859. THE BAT-
TLE'S THOUSANDS OF WOUNDED SOLDIERS INSPIRED HENRI DUNANT
TO LAUNCH A MOVEMENT THAT WOULD LEAD TO THE FORMATION OF
THE RED CROSS.

to have their wounds dressed and to receive food and water.

Dunant turned his memories of those events into a
best-selling book, *A Memory of Solferino*. He ended the
book with a question: "Would it not be possible, in time of

peace and quiet, to form relief societies for the purpose of having care given to the wounded in wartime by zealous, devoted and thoroughly qualified volunteers?"

This question led to the founding of the International Red Cross. Dunant asked another question in his book: Could military authorities of different European nations find a way to create a set of principles for caring for the wounded in wartime? This second question turned out to be the basis for the Geneva Conventions.

The First Convention

The Geneva Conventions are a series of treaties among nations created in Geneva, Switzerland, beginning in 1864. Their purpose is to provide guidelines for the treatment of men and women who are wounded in war, of prisoners of war, and of civilians in time of war. They are generally grouped together with treaties formulated in The Hague, the capital of The Netherlands.

Together, these treaties—they are also known as agreements or accords—set the standards for international humanitarian law. The treaties address the laws and customs of war for all countries, and nearly all of the world's nations have accepted and ratified them.

The First Geneva Convention, inspired by Dunant, began with the formation of a group of five people in 1863. Later, this group became known as the International Committee of the Red Cross. The committee helped gather representatives from sixteen European nations in Geneva, Switzerland.

There, they designed a treaty to help save lives, provide relief for the wounded, and protect the civilians who would provide that relief. The First Geneva Convention treaty was signed on August 22, 1864. Later, nearly all nations signed on, including the United States in 1882.

POW Concerns

The First Geneva Convention dealt with the care of sick and wounded soldiers. It did not address prisoners of war specifically. But it did lay the foundation for future conventions that would deal with POWs. The first Convention was important for another reason. It established the worldwide humanitarian aid organization known as the International Red Cross and Red Crescent Movement:

> **A distinctive and uniform flag shall be adopted for hospitals, ambulances and evacuations. It must, on every occasion, be accompanied by the national flag. An arm-badge (brassard) shall also be allowed for individuals neutralized . . . .**

> **The flag and the arm-badge shall bear a red cross on a white ground.**

In later years, the International Red Cross would play a crucial role in the care of POWs. It would monitor their treatment, inspect the living conditions in their camps, and work with the Detaining Power to improve prisoners' lives.

The Hague Convention of 1907

The first treaty that mentioned prisoners of war took place in The Hague in 1907. It was called Convention (IV) Respecting the Laws and Customs of War on Land. One chapter dealt specifically with the rights of prisoners of war. These passages show how the convention addressed four of the basic POW rights:

Basic Needs "[P]risoners of war shall be treated as regards board, lodging, and clothing on the same footing as the troops of the Government who captured them."

Humanitarian Aid "Relief societies for prisoners of war . . . shall receive . . . every facility for the efficient performance of their humane task. . . . Agents of these societies may be admitted to the places of internment for the purpose of distributing relief."

Labor "The State may utilize the labor of prisoners of war according to their rank and aptitude, officers excepted. The tasks shall not be excessive and shall have no connection with the operations of the war."

Repatriation "After the conclusion of peace, the repatriation of prisoners of war shall be carried out as quickly as possible."

Now that these laws and customs of war were set down and agreed upon by the world's nations, how faithfully would warring armies honor them? Would prisoners of war really receive better treatment in wars to come?

4
Battlefield Realities

The first big test for the Geneva and Hague treaties was the world's first global war. On one side were the Allied Powers of France, Great Britain, Italy, Russia, Serbia, Japan, and the United States. On the other side were the Central Powers of Germany and Austria-Hungary.

World War I was a long and bloody war. More than 8 million soldiers were killed and more than 21 million wounded. About 6.6 million were taken prisoner.

A Convenient Excuse

How well were these prisoners treated? Overcrowded quarters, mediocre food at best, poor sanitary facilities, attacks of vermin and contagious diseases, hard work in unhealthy and dangerous environments—these conditions proved to be the rule instead of the exception.

Certainly humane treatment as outlined in the treaties was the ideal. But in this war it often remained just that: an ideal. As in the U.S. Civil War, shortage of funds and other realities of war kept getting in the way.

THIS PHOTOGRAPH FROM WORLD WAR I SHOWS RED CROSS WORKERS CARING FOR WOUNDED FRENCH SOLDIERS. THE DISTINCTIVE RED CROSS MARKINGS ON ARMBANDS AND AMBULANCES HELPED KEEP THE WORKERS SAFE FROM HARM AS THEY DID THEIR HUMANITARIAN WORK.

It had been hoped that the 1907 Hague Convention would improve conditions considerably for prisoners of war, but evidently it had not. Too late, the treaty's shortcomings became clear. While it was well-meaning, the treaty was muddy and vague where it should have been clear and definite.

The 1907 Hague Convention had not gone far enough. Prisoners of war "must be humanely treated," the treaty declared. But it neither defined *humane* nor gave any concrete examples of humane treatment. This left the detaining powers with a convenient excuse. They could claim that the substandard conditions in their camps met *their* definition of humane.

THIS **1916** PHOTO SHOWS PRISONERS OUTSIDE A COOK HOUSE IN A POW CAMP IN TURKEY. THE TUBS ARE FILLED WITH LOAVES OF FLAT BREAD, THE VERY BASIC, NO-FRILLS SORT OF FOOD THAT MOST WORLD WAR I PRISONERS RECEIVED.

The 1929 Geneva Convention

The ICRC proposed that a more complete and precise treaty be created. The result was the Geneva Convention (III) Relative to the Treatment of Prisoners of War, a treaty signed by the United States and forty-six other countries in Geneva, Switzerland, on July 27, 1929.

The participants were determined to make this treaty clearer and more precise than its predecessor. This treaty was about 10,000 words long, compared to only about 1,200 in the 1907 Hague treaty. It dealt with the

same basic rights as that earlier treaty but in greater detail—
and added some new rights as well. Here are examples.

Humane Treatment. The 1907 treaty said only that
prisoners must be humanely treated. The 1929 treaty
stated: "They must at all times be humanely treated and
protected, particularly against acts of violence, insults
and public curiosity. Measures of reprisal against them
are prohibited."

The 1907 treaty did not deal with the issue of using
prisoners as human shields. The 1929 treaty stated
"No prisoner may, at any time, be . . . used to give protection from bombardment to certain points or certain
regions by his presence."

The 1907 treaty did not mention interrogation
methods. The 1929 treaty stated: "No coercion may be
used on prisoners to secure information as to the condition
of their army or country. Prisoners who refuse to answer
may not be threatened, insulted, or exposed to unpleasant
or disadvantageous treatment of any kind whatever."

Dignity and Honor. The 1907 treaty did not deal with
this issue at all. The 1929 treaty stated: "Prisoners of war
have the right to have their person and their honor re-
spected. Women shall be treated with all the regard due to
their sex."

Medical Attention. The 1907 treaty made no mention
of this issue in regard to prisoners of war. The 1929 treaty
stated: "Every camp shall have an infirmary, where prisoners of war shall receive every kind of attention they need. If
necessary, isolated quarters shall be reserved for the sick
affected with contagious diseases."

Basic Needs. The 1907 treaty made only this general
statement: "[P]risoners of war shall be treated as regards
board, lodging, and clothing on the same footing as the
troops of the Government who captured them." The 1929

The Life of a British POW

The diaries of World War I prisoners paint a grim picture of conditions and daily life in the camps. The following passages were written by Private Reginald Morris, a British POW captured by the Germans. The POW camp was located in France, which Germany occupied at the time.

There were a few hundred of us at this camp at Marchiennes. It was a cheerless place . . . designed to break the best of hearts.

We had to sleep on a stone floor. If a small quantity of straw could be got, and what is more important, kept, the coldness of this floor could be modified. Straw could only be kept by sitting on it; as soon as your back was turned, it was taken by your neighboring bedmates.

At night, if the air was very cold, we lay and froze until, becoming numbed, we were forced to get up and walk about the yard for an hour or so to try and keep warm. . . .

Lice, also, began to appear and became a continual source of irritation. They remained from this time onwards my constant and faithful companions until my release. Water for washing purposes was unobtainable. We had no blankets. . . .

We were made to work, and were sent out in large working parties. After breakfast, we set out before it was light, and seemed to walk miles through deserted and shell-smashed villages. . . .

It was heavy and heart-breaking work on the little food we were given. The tramp to the neighborhood of our work was in itself a task. . . . Sometimes we had to carry on under fire from our own guns. . . . When relieved we tramped home, it being generally dark when we arrived. . . . Then we had our dinner. Dinner! let those two syllables sink in. Dinner! all the whole day between 5 in the morning and 5 in the evening, we had nothing whatever to eat.

treaty went into detail on prisoners' rights to food, drinking water, clothing and bedding, sanitary facilities, and physical exercise.

Humanitarian Aid. The 1907 treaty stated that representatives of relief societies, such as the ICRC, "may be admitted to the places of internment for the purpose of distributing relief." Notice how much more detailed and forceful the wording of the 1929 treaty was: "Representatives of the Protecting Power or its accepted delegates shall be permitted to go to any place, without exception, where prisoners of war are interned. They shall have access to all places occupied by prisoners and may interview them, as a general rule without witnesses, personally or through interpreters."

Labor. The new treaty was more detailed and forceful on this issue as well. 1907: "The State may utilize the labor of prisoners of war according to their rank and aptitude, officers excepted. The tasks shall not be excessive and shall have no connection with the operations of the war." 1929: "Labor furnished by prisoners of war shall have no direct relation with war operations. It is especially prohibited to use prisoners for manufacturing and transporting arms or munitions of any kind or for transporting material intended for combatant units.

"It is forbidden to use prisoners of war at unhealthful or dangerous work."

Once again the stage was set. How would warring armies react to these new, more definite and detailed laws and customs of war? The world would soon find out.

5
Rewards and Punishments

The second global war came just twenty-one years after the first. It would prove to be the biggest and deadliest armed conflict in human history. World War II pitted the Axis Powers—Germany, Italy, and Japan—against the Allied Powers, led by Great Britain, the Soviet Union, and the United States. It would end with the United States dropping two atomic bombs on Japan.

Do Unto Others

General Dwight D. Eisenhower commanded the Allied forces in Europe, while Nazi Party leader and dictator Adolf Hitler was Germany's commander in chief. After the war, General Eisenhower was asked why Allied forces had followed the 1929 Geneva Convention so strictly and treated German prisoners of war so well.

Eisenhower gave two reasons for this humane treatment. "[I]n the first place," he said, "my country was required to do so by the terms of the Geneva Convention. In the second place, the Germans had some thousands of

American and British prisoners and I did not want to give Hitler the excuse or justification for treating our prisoners more harshly than he was already doing."

Eisenhower's first reason had to do with duty. It was the Allied nations' responsibility to comply since they had ratified the convention on the rights of prisoners of war. This was the purely moral and ethical reason: When you make a promise you are bound to keep it.

His second reason was more practical and pragmatic. The key was reciprocity: a promise of equal treatment. The Golden Rule is, "And as ye would that men should do to you, do ye also to them likewise." (Luke 6:31) This is the Christian version. The same advice appears in many of the world's religions. In Confucianism, it goes: "Do not do to others what you do not want them to do to you." And in Islam, it reads, "None of you [truly] believes until he wishes for his brother what he wishes for himself."

Advantages of Humane Treatment

In the case of German prisoners of war held by Allied forces, the Golden Rule applied this way: when you see us treating your prisoners humanely, you will be more likely to treat ours humanely. The principle of reciprocity applies in reverse as well. President Lincoln recognized this when he issued Order 233. That order turned the Golden Rule on its head by sending this message to the Confederate Army: A government that fails to comply with accepted standards of humane treatment for POWs puts its own combatants in danger of being similarly mistreated: You abuse our soldiers and we will abuse yours.

Following the 1929 Geneva Convention's conditions for humane treatment offers other advantages. Showing POWs respect and keeping them healthy gave the detaining power a cooperative work force that could ease their own soldiers' burdens by doing jobs such as construction and cleaning.

Then there was the surrender advantage. Word got around that the Allies were treating German POWs in line with the 1929 Geneva Convention. After the war, General Eisenhower made a report to Congress. In it he revealed that a large number of German soldiers had surrendered because they had known that they would be well-treated in the Allied camps.

Troop morale was yet another advantage. Following the convention's mandates meant that Allied soldiers knew their side's prisoners were being treated humanely, even when the enemy did not reciprocate. Allied soldiers were then able to look upon their side with pride as morally superior to the enemy.

A Camp in Arizona

Exactly how did a POW camp go about honoring prisoners' rights? When U.S. troops entered the war, following the 1941 Japanese attack on Pearl Harbor, Hawaii, Americans hardly had any direct experience with POWs. During World War I, only about 1,300 enemy prisoners were held captive in the United States.

But during World War II, that number mushroomed to 425,000. Nearly seven hundred camps had to be built to house them all. Most camps went up in rural areas far from heavy population centers, factories, and military bases where the prisoners might pose a security threat. And most were constructed in the warm climates of the South and Southwest, where the cost of heating barracks could be kept low.

One such camp was built in Florence, Arizona. A penitentiary already existed in the remote little town east of Phoenix, but Article 56 of the 1929 Geneva Convention prohibited the use of prisons to house POWs.

PRISONERS ON A WORK DETAIL AT THE FLORENCE, ARIZONA, INTERNMENT CAMP PLANT CROPS THAT WILL LATER SUPPLY PEOPLE IN THE UNITED STATES WITH FRESH, NUTRITIOUS PRODUCE.

So a camp was built from scratch in Florence, a vast camp that included a bakery, hospital, movie theaters, basketball courts—even a swimming pool. The two-story wooden barracks had broad overhangs along both floors to hold back the Arizona sun's blazing heat. Twenty-six guard towers surrounded the grounds.

Welcome to Prison

The Florence camp was completed just in time to accommodate prisoners from the war's largest mass surrender, which came in the spring of 1943. That's when U.S. and British troops routed German and Italian troops from hills along the northern coast of Tunisia, North Africa. Within two weeks a quarter-million Axis soldiers had emerged from their fighting positions in the hills to lay down their arms and surrender.

Thousands of the Italian prisoners were shipped to Florence, filling the camp to capacity. Upon arrival, each prisoner found a welcoming letter written by the U.S. camp commander, translated into Italian.

Here is the English version. Notice how the letter keeps referring to laws and customs from the 1929 Geneva Convention. To help point this out, passages from the convention have been added, in italics.

From the camp letter: Permit me to welcome you to this camp. Due to the fortunes of war, you find yourselves detained by the Army of the United States of America. . . . You have my full assurance that you will at all times be humanely treated and protected, particularly against acts of violence, insults and public curiosity.

From the 1929 Geneva Convention: *They must at all times be humanely treated and protected,*

particularly against acts of violence, insults and public curiosity."

As a soldier and as a camp commander, I advise and urge you to preserve your morale. You can best do this by taking advantage of the opportunities afforded you to correspond with your family . . .

"*As soon as possible, every prisoner must be enabled to correspond with his family himself.*"

by keeping your person and your quarters scrupulously clean . . .

"*Prisoners of war shall be lodged in buildings or in barracks affording all possible guarantees of hygiene and healthfulness.*"

by attending religious services and, very important, by preserving a serene disposition at all times.

"*Prisoners of war shall enjoy complete liberty in the exercise of their religion, including attendance at the services of their faiths.*"

You are still soldiers of the Kingdom of Italy and your civil status is protected.

"*Prisoners retain their civil status.*"

You are not confined or detained as punishment.

"*Measures of reprisal against them are prohibited.*"

42

It is my duty to detain each of you until properly released. Outside of the detention features of your stay here, you will be cared for on a basis comparable to the care given to soldiers of the United States of America.

"[C]onditions shall be the same as for the troops at base camps of the Detaining Power."

How did the Italian POWs respond to this kind of treatment after months and years of fighting in the hills of North Africa? The letters they wrote home to loved ones sometimes sounded more like letters from happy vacationers:

The voyage here was delightful and I find myself with many friends in Arizona, land of dreams and illusions!

We are enjoying the utmost cleanliness and comfort. In addition, the food is really marvelous, just to give you an idea of what we eat, here is the menu for today's breakfast: chocolate, toast, butter & honey; dinner: spaghetti, potato salad, salami, cheese and dessert.

Race and Reciprocity

Germany had signed the 1929 Geneva Convention, but it was race that determined how the Germans treated their Allied POWs. U.S. and British subjects probably got the best treatment. The worst went to the Polish soldiers taken prisoner when Hitler's troops invaded and occupied Poland. Hitler had a hierarchy of races, arranged from top to bottom, with the lower-end races marked for extermination.

Near the very bottom rung of Hitler's racial ladder were the Poles. The Russians were down there too, along with anyone of Jewish descent. That's why Polish and Russian prisoners were often neglected, mistreated, or murdered by their German captors.

Reciprocity meant German prisoners paid a price as well. Since the Germans were being so brutal with Russian prisoners, the Soviets felt justified in brutalizing German prisoners. So captives from both sides suffered inhumane treatment.

Japan: Noncompliance

Japan had not signed the 1929 Geneva Convention. But they assured the ICRC that they would apply the Geneva rules to captured members of the Allied armed forces. The Japanese did not live up to their promise.

The Bataan Peninsula is on West Luzon Island in the Philippines. It was April 1943 and Allied forces on the peninsula were running out of food and ammunition. They realized they could not survive much longer. So on April 9, they laid down their weapons, raised white flags, and emerged from their defensive positions to give themselves up.

In all, about 75,000 Filipino and U.S. troops surrendered at Bataan. They presented a serious problem for the Japanese, who needed to move them to a camp but had no vehicles to transport them. Therefore, the prisoners had to walk. It was a forced march of 70 miles in humid weather under a hot sun.

The Allied prisoners were in bad health to begin with, and they got little food and water on the way. It wasn't long before prisoners began falling back and dying, either from lack of food and water or from the force of an executioner's bullet. Japanese troops were under orders to kill any prisoners who fell behind.

A small part of the journey was by train. Crowded into suffocating boxcars, more prisoners died on board. It took a week to reach the camp. By then, 10,000 of the Bataan POWs had perished.

General Douglas MacArthur was supreme commander of Allied forces in the Southwest Pacific area. He wrote that "soldiers of an army invariably reflect the attitude of their general. The leader is the essence. . . . [W]idespread and continuing abuse can only be a fixed responsibility of highest field authority."

After the war, Lieutenant General Masaharu Homma went on trial before a U.S. military commission in Manila, Philippines, for war crimes committed by troops under his command during the Bataan Death March. On the morning of April 3, 1946, a firing squad ended his life.

War Crimes

Lieutenant General Masaharu Homma was only one of thousands of former Japanese military leaders tried for war crimes involving POWs. The trials were held during 1947 and 1948 in various Asian cities, including Tokyo, Japan. Some of those convicted received prison sentences. Others, such as Masaharu, were executed.

But it was the war crime trials of Nazi officials that attracted most of the world's attention. Nazi forces had exterminated some six million Jewish civilians. They had executed millions more civilians and prisoners of war. The world was waiting to hear what they had to say about their crimes and then to see them punished.

The trials were held in Nuremberg, Germany, from 1945 to 1949. Each defendant had legal counsel and an opportunity to testify in his own defense. Some were accused of mistreating prisoners of war.

One of these men was Joachim von Ribbentrop, Hitler's foreign minister. Von Ribbentrop was also accused

Factories of Death

War can bring out the very best in people: kindness, courage, self-sacrifice. It can also bring out the very worst.

In Japanese, *maruta* means "logs of wood." That's what the members of Unit 731 called the Allied prisoners of war brought to them as experimental subjects.

The scientists in this secret biological warfare unit were able to observe the results of controlled experiments they never could have performed on humans in peacetime. There were no limits. Everything was permitted in their research facilities, which became known as factories of death.

The Unit 731 scientists infected prisoners with plague, cholera, anthrax, and typhoid. They siphoned out their blood and replaced it with the blood of horses. Prisoners were bombarded with lethal doses of X-rays, whirled to death in giant centrifuges, sealed in high-pressure chambers until their eyes popped from their sockets. They were electrocuted, dehydrated, frozen, scorched with flamethrowers, boiled alive.

In May 1945, Unit 731 scientists received a special batch of *maruta*: eight American airmen who had been shot down over southern Japan. While the prisoners were still alive, scientists dissected them organ by organ.

At the war's end, with Japan defeated, the Unit 731 scientists and their families, some 2,000 in all, fled their factories of death and scattered. But not before one final atrocity. They opened up laboratory cages and set free thousands of infected rats.

EXECUTION WAS A QUICK WAY OF REMOVING THE BURDEN OF CARING FOR PRISONERS OF WAR. HERE, A JAPANESE EXECUTIONER IS ABOUT TO COMMIT A WAR CRIME BY BEHEADING AN ALLIED PRISONER.

THERE WERE ELEVEN NUREMBERG TRIALS IN ALL. IN THE DOCTORS TRIAL, TWENTY-THREE NAZI PHYSICIANS WERE CHARGED WITH CONDUCTING INHUMAN MEDICAL EXPERIMENTS. HERE, HITLER'S PERSONAL PHYSICIAN, KARL BRANDT, LISTENS TO A JUDGE SENTENCE HIM TO DEATH BY HANGING. THE SENTENCE WAS CARRIED OUT IN **1948.**

of playing a key role in arranging for Jews to be deported to Nazi extermination camps. As to prisoners of war, he claimed that he had never had any POWs harmed. In fact, he insisted, "I have always advocated the observance of the Geneva Convention."

The court did not believe Von Ribbentrop's defense and found him guilty of war crimes. He was sentenced to death by hanging. The sentence was carried out on the night of October 16, 1946.

The Nuremberg trials did more than punish these men.

The trials were held in an open court, where reporters from around the world could see and hear everything. That way the trials exposed Nazi officials to public view and helped reveal the horrendous extent of their crimes against combatants, civilians, and prisoners of war.

6
A New Set of Rights

During the early years of World War II, national leaders realized that the world had become an extremely dangerous place. Germany, Italy, and Japan now threatened to dominate the entire planet. These threats called for new national policies.

On August 14, 1941, U.S. President Franklin D. Roosevelt and British Prime Minister Winston S. Churchill met on board warships off the coast of Newfoundland. Together, they fashioned an historic document that helped launch an international humanitarian movement. This document, known as the Atlantic Charter, stated:

> **The President and the Prime Minister have . . . considered the dangers to world civilization arising from the policies of military domination by conquest upon which the Hitlerite government of Germany and other governments have embarked . . . and have made clear the steps which their countries are respectively taking for their safety in the face of these dangers.**

And so they "deem it right to make known certain common principles in the national policies of their respective countries on which they base their hopes for a better future for the world."

Revolutionary Ideals

First, nations must do all they can to keep from using force in their international relations. They should use force only as a last resort, in self-defense, or when authorized to use it by the community of world nations. Second, nations must respect the inherent dignity and equal and inalienable rights of everyone. Finally, they should work to promote economic progress through free trade.

The idea of nations joining together to keep the peace and respect human dignity must have seemed an implausible goal then, with Nazi Germany on a full-fledged offensive in Europe and the Holocaust raging: a dim ray of hope in a very dark world. But when the war was over, the Atlantic Charter and its principles would point the way toward the founding of the United Nations (UN).

This international organization describes itself as a global association of governments. When it was founded in 1945, a month after the war's end, the UN's member nations numbered 50. As of 2006, 192 nations belonged: nearly all the world's independent states.

On December 10, 1948, the UN issued a historic document of its own, the Universal Declaration of Human Rights. The declaration reminded the world's nations what they had just been through: two world wars and the Holocaust, "barbarous acts which have outraged the conscience of mankind."

The declaration announced that people were now looking forward to "a world in which human beings shall enjoy freedom of speech and belief and freedom from fear and want as the highest aspiration of the common peo-

ELEANOR ROOSEVELT, WORLDWIDE LECTURER AND WRITER, HOLDS A UNIVERSAL DECLARATION OF HUMAN RIGHTS POSTER IN 1949. SHE WAS A MORE FERVENT CHAMPION OF HUMAN RIGHTS THAN HER HUSBAND, PRESIDENT FRANKLIN D. ROOSEVELT. SHE WAS AGAINST THE INTERNMENT OF THE JAPANESE AMERICANS IN WORLD WAR II AND A TIRELESS CAMPAIGNER FOR EQUAL RIGHTS.

ple." It anticipated a world in which "human rights should be protected by the rule of law" so that "man is not to be compelled to have recourse, as a last resort, to rebellion against tyranny and oppression."

This UN declaration did more than merely state these ideals as hopes for the future. It urged humankind to use the document

> as a common standard of achievement for all peoples and all nations, to the end that every

individual and every organ of society . . . shall strive by teaching and education to promote respect for these rights and freedoms and by progressive measures, national and international, to secure their universal and effective recognition and observance.

POWs Redefined

After two withering world wars, hope for humanitarian progress had blossomed anew. What would this optimistic climate mean for prisoners of war?

It would help spur the world's nations to once again revisit the Geneva Conventions and deal with a new set of problems. By now there were four separate conventions. The third convention was the one covering POWs: The Convention Relative to the Treatment of Prisoners of War. Once again, it was expanded. The 1929 version was about 10,000 words long. This new 1949 version was more than 23,000 words long.

The new version of the Third Convention took into account trends from World War II that the 1929 version could not have foreseen. One was the resistance movements in Poland, France, Holland, Denmark, and all the other nations invaded by Nazi Germany.

Civilians in these Nazi-occupied nations gathered together to form secret, underground groups dedicated to resisting the Nazis by whatever means possible. They refused to cooperate with their occupiers. They hid Allied pilots whose planes had crashed and helped them escape back to Allied countries. They even formed their own invasion units to recapture towns from the Nazis.

To deal with this new type of combatant, the 1949 Convention broadened the categories of persons entitled to prisoner-of-war status. They now included members of resistance movements, both organized and spontaneous.

Prisoners' Rights Redefined

The 1949 Third Convention also redefined some prisoner-of-war rights in light of what had taken place during the war.

Humane Treatment. The horrors suffered by prisoners in Soviet, German, and Japanese camps, along with Unit 731's ghastly medical experiments, led to these new paragraphs. For the first time, the word *torture* was used.

> Every prisoner of war, when questioned on the subject, is bound to give only his surname, first name and rank, date of birth, and army, regimental, personal or serial number . . .

> No physical or mental torture, nor any other form of coercion, may be inflicted on prisoners of war to secure from them information of any kind whatever. Prisoners of war who refuse to answer may not be threatened, insulted, or exposed to unpleasant or disadvantageous treatment of any kind.

> In particular, no prisoner of war may be subjected to physical mutilation or to medical or scientific experiments of any kind which are not justified by the medical, dental or hospital treatment of the prisoner concerned and carried out in his interest.

Dignity and Honor. The 1949 Third Geneva Convention also stated that prisoners of war

> shall in all circumstances be treated humanely, without any adverse distinction founded on race, colour, religion or faith, sex, birth or wealth, or any other similar criteria. To this end the following

acts are and shall remain prohibited at any time
and in any place whatsoever with respect to the
above-mentioned persons:

(a) violence to life and person, in particular murder
of all kinds, mutilation, cruel treatment and torture;

(b) taking of hostages;

(c) outrages upon personal dignity, in particular,
humiliating and degrading treatment.

Legal Rights. Also forbidden were

the passing of sentences and the carrying out of
executions without previous judgment pronounced
by a regularly constituted court affording all the
judicial guarantees which are recognized as indispensable by civilized peoples.

Basic Needs. The unhealthy conditions of most of these
camps led to changes in the laws. The 1929 Third Convention said only: "The food ration of prisoners of war shall
be equal in quantity and quality to that of troops at
base camps." The 1949 Convention stated: "The basic
daily food rations shall be sufficient in quantity, quality
and variety to keep prisoners of war in good health and
to prevent loss of weight or the development of nutri-
tional deficiencies."

Humanitarian Aid. POW camps needed to keep better
track of the prisoners being held there and to better com-
municate their whereabouts to the outside world. And
after the war's end, what about soldiers who never return
home but whose bodies are never found? Were they killed

in action? Or did they die in prisoner of war camps? Families and loved ones need to know. So the following directive was added:

A Central Prisoners of War Information Agency shall be created in a neutral country. The International Committee of the Red Cross shall, if it deems necessary, propose to the Powers concerned the organization of such an Agency.

The function of the Agency shall be to collect all the information it may obtain through official or private channels respecting prisoners of war, and to transmit it as rapidly as possible to the country of origin of the prisoners of war or to the Power on which they depend.

To help in the collection of information, an identity document known as a capture card was mandated for each prisoner:

Each Party to a conflict is required to furnish the persons under its jurisdiction who are liable to become prisoners of war, with an identity card showing the owner's surname, first names, rank, army, regimental, personal or serial number or equivalent information, and date of birth. . . . As far as possible the card shall measure 6.5 x 10 cm and shall be issued in duplicate. The identity card shall be shown by the prisoner of war upon demand, but may in no case be taken away from him.

A copy of the card was to be filed within seven days after the prisoner's arrival at the camp. A well-run camp would have copies of these cards on file for humanitarian aid representatives to consult.

Repatriation. The 1783 Treaty of Paris, which officially ended the American Revolutionary War, stated: "All prisoners on both sides shall be set at liberty." Rather than return to Europe, thousands of British soldiers, as well as German soldiers who had fought for the British, chose to remain in the United States and become part of the new nation.

THIS **1942** PHOTO SHOWS SOVIET SOLDIERS TAKING GERMAN SOL-DIERS PRISONER. AFTER THE WAR ENDED, IN **1945**, THE SOVIETS KEPT SOME OF THESE PRISONERS FOR USE AS SLAVE LABORERS.

Those soldiers were exceptions to the rule. Before World War II, repatriation was a fairly simple matter. It was common practice to exchange prisoners at the end of a conflict. Then the prisoners would return home. Repatriation at war's end was every prisoner's right.

One nation did not follow the practice of repatriation at the end of World War II. The Soviet Union hung on to a large number of Japanese and German prisoners. The Soviet government, led by totalitarian dictator Joseph Stalin, used them as slave laborers to help repair the damage done to the Soviet Union during the war.

The statement on repatriation from the 1929 Convention read: "[R]epatriation of prisoners shall be effected with the least possible delay after the conclusion." Because of the Soviets, this statement needed strengthening. That's why the delegates to the 1949 Convention changed "with the least possible delay" to "without delay."

The 1949 (Third) Geneva Convention helped strengthen the rights of prisoners of war. But, like the conventions before it, this version would soon need revising.

7
Repatriation and Propaganda

The first big test of the 1949 Third Convention was not long in coming. The Korean War (1950–1953) was a direct result of political and geographic changes that took place at the end of World War II.

The United States and the Soviet Union emerged from the war as dueling superpowers. Each nation came away with roughly half of the Korean Peninsula to hold in trust until a new Korean government could be formed. South Korea went to the United States, North Korea to the Soviets.

It was not long before the two superpowers were deeply involved in a civil war between the two Koreas. Helped by the United Nations, the United States supported the South Korean army with troops and supplies. Communist China and the Soviet Union did the same for the army of North Korea.

To some people this looked more like a war between the two superpowers than a civil war. There were the United States and its allies on one side and the Communist powers of the Soviet Union and the People's Republic of China on the other: democracy versus communism.

The Repatriation Issue

The conflict between the two superpowers was already heating up at the end of World War II. Soviet behavior toward prisoners of war was one reason why. First, there was the Soviet decision at the war's end to deny prisoners their right to repatriation and hold on to them for slave labor.

But the Soviets committed an even more serious violation of the Third Convention, which came as a shocking surprise to the United States. America and the Soviet

THESE NORTH KOREAN PRISONERS OF WAR SIT WITH CARDS AROUND THEIR NECKS THAT DETAIL THEIR INDIVIDUAL HISTORIES. THEY ARE WAITING TO BE PROCESSED AND TAKEN TO CAMPS.

Union were allies during the war, but some Soviet prisoners had fallen into U.S. hands. That's why at war's end the United States repatriated them to their homeland, in line with the Geneva Convention.

This turned out to be a disastrous move. U.S. officials had forgotten that totalitarian governments had a habit of turning their own citizens into enemies. A number of these repatriated Soviet prisoners had fallen out of favor with their totalitarian leaders. Some were condemned for the simple act of surrendering. Instead of welcoming home all its returning soldiers, the Soviet government imprisoned some and executed others.

North Korea also had a communist, totalitarian government that might not look kindly upon its repatriated prisoners. Many had surrendered. If sent back home, would they too be imprisoned or executed? U.S. officials were determined not to make the same mistake again.

Officials from the United Nations and North Korea were working on a settlement to end the war. As part of that settlement, the UN side proposed that repatriation be strictly voluntary, even though this went against the Third Convention. At war's end, it was suggested that all prisoners on both sides should be free to choose whether or not to return to their homelands.

A Propaganda Blow

At first the Communists rejected this proposal. The reason was a survey the UN had taken. It asked prisoners of war held by South Korea whether they wished to return to their homeland at war's end. The south held about 170,000 POWs in all, some from North Korea, the rest from Communist China. Of these, only 70,000 wished to return to their communist homeland. The rest, nearly 100,000, did not want to be repatriated.

In the societies of Communist China and the Soviet Union, propaganda was a key weapon. They had a cause to promote: worldwide communism. How they looked to the rest of the world's nations was vitally important. The rulers had to seem strong and determined, and the people had to appear dedicated to their cause and happy to be living in a communist society.

So when the United Nations showed North Korea and Communist China the results of the POW survey, it came as a sharp propaganda blow. Those communist nations did not want to let it be revealed that so many of their soldiers did not want to return home.

But then South Korea made a move that helped turn the tide. It released 25,000 North Korean POWs who had elected to refuse repatriation. But the South Koreans called the release a massive prison breakout.

The North Korean government welcomed this "breakout." It allowed them to save face by not having to publicly admit that all those thousands of "escaped" prisoners did not want to return home. Finally, the North Koreans agreed to a cease-fire settlement that included voluntary repatriation.

A Slaughterhouse

North Korea had agreed to abide by the 1949 Geneva Convention (III) Relative to the Treatment of Prisoners of War. But by no stretch of the imagination could the treatment that U.S. POWs received in North Korean camps be called humane.

Of the 7,140 U.S. soldiers taken prisoner during the war, more than 2,400 did not survive their stay in the North Korean camps. That adds up to a death rate of about 38 percent, the highest percentage of U.S. POW deaths of any conflict during the war-torn twentieth century.

THESE U.S. SOLDIERS WERE CAPTURED BY NORTH KOREAN FORCES
IN 1951.

Contributing to the death rate were the poor dietary and sanitary conditions in the camps, combined with inadequate medical care and brutal mistreatment. Author and journalist Laurence Jolidon worked as a war correspondent during the conflict. In his book on U.S. prisoners in the Korean War, Jolidon compared life in the camps to a slaughterhouse. "The cruelty was astounding," he wrote. "If you survived a death march to get to a camp, there was nothing there—no food, no medicine, no clothing."

Brainwashing

Communist China also agreed to abide by the 1949 Geneva Convention on POWs—with certain exceptions. One was the use of a set of coercive techniques on prisoners. The Chinese called this their "Lenient Policy." The popular term was "brainwashing."

Brainwashing is not a form of interrogation. It is a relentless physical and psychological process whose primary aim is to "reform" or "re-educate" the prisoner: to get him to see things from the point of view of his captors, to believe what they believe. The Chinese communists also used brainwashing to make prisoners more cooperative and less likely to resist their captors or attempt escape.

Brainwashing techniques included threatening the prisoner with physical abuse, keeping him confined, and withholding food and sleep for long periods of time. Meanwhile, he had to listen as his captors repeatedly told him things such as, "You are not here to defend freedom. You are a bad person. You are in pain. Agree with me that you are bad and in pain."

Gradually, the prisoner became more and more disoriented. He lost his bearings, his sense of who he was. Both he himself and the world around him came to seem strange and uncertain.

At this point in the brainwashing process his captors started telling him, "I can help you. You can help yourself. It's not your fault. It's your beliefs. You can change them. You can choose good. You can become a new person."

Some prisoners pretended to snap under brainwashing and adopt communist beliefs. They did this to avoid physical abuse. Others snapped temporarily but later recovered. Only a few prisoners did not recover. A total of twenty-one U.S. prisoners of war refused repatriation at the end of the war and chose to live in North Korea or Communist China instead.

8
Dignity and Humiliation

The similarities between the Vietnam and Korean wars are remarkable. Both were fought within the borders of what had once been a single, troubled Asian nation. And the world community divided each nation into two separate nations.

In both cases the division was intended to be temporary. These separate half-nations, each with its own government, were expected to hold democratic elections that would reunify them.

But before elections could take place, the two halves aligned themselves with competing world powers. This was the Cold War era, which ran from the late 1940s to the early 1990s. North Vietnam, like North Korea, became a communist nation supported by the Soviet Union and Communist China. South Vietnam, like South Korea, sided with the United States.

These alignments led to an outbreak of civil war in the

two Vietnams, as it had in the two Koreas. The Korean War resulted in two permanently divided nations. The Vietnam War led to a different result. After U.S. troops left Vietnam in 1973, the war continued for two more years. Then the soldiers of the north, known as the Viet Cong, overran the south, and the two Vietnams became a single nation: the Socialist Republic of Vietnam.

Interrogation and Torture

The governments of both Vietnams had signed the 1949 Geneva Convention on POWs. But neither one got high marks for honoring POW rights. Both the North and South Vietnamese were notorious for exposing prisoners to inhumane conditions, including torture.

John McCain recalls his ordeals during the early days of his captivity. The 1949 Convention stated that he was legally bound to give his Viet Cong captors only his name, rank, serial number, and date of birth. And that was what he did, again and again.

But his interrogators kept demanding more. They would ask for military information, such as what new targets were to be hit and when more missions would be flown. Each time McCain refused to answer, his interrogator would smash his face and head, eventually knocking him unconscious.

Accounts of surviving American POWs show just how tough it was to emerge from captivity alive. Some prisoners died from wounds sustained in combat that went untreated and became infected. Others perished from their captors' systematic beatings. One survivor recalls the ominous words with which a Viet Cong prison guard welcomed him to his new cell: "It's easy to die but hard to live," he was told, "and we'll show you just how hard it is to live."

Heartbreak Hotel

Like other close-knit groups, POWs come to develop their own colorful language. The North Vietnamese capital of Hanoi used four of the city's penitentiaries as POW camps—a violation of the 1949 Convention. To the POWs, they were known as the Plantation, the Zoo, Alcatraz, and the Hanoi Hilton—sarcastically named after the worldwide luxury hotel chain.

From the so-called Hanoi Hilton (actually Hoa Lo Prison) come some of the most brutal stories of prison life in North Vietnam. This was the country's main penitentiary, taking up an entire city block in the middle of Hanoi. A massive concrete wall 16 feet high and 6 feet thick surrounded the complex. Shards of broken glass ran along the top where three strands of barbed wire tilted out and downward toward the street. At each of the four corners, mounted atop the wall, a guard tower loomed. It was no wonder the Hilton had an escape-proof reputation.

The POWs also had their own names for the rooms inside. There was the Meathook Room, Heartbreak Hotel, and the Knobby Room. The last got its name from the knobs all over the walls. Each one was the size of a clenched fist and made of acoustical plaster to help absorb the tortured men's screams.

And the living conditions? Everett Alvarez Jr. was a U.S. Navy flyer who spent time in a Hanoi Hilton cell. Among Alvarez's scarier memories were his cellmates—rats the size of cats. Memories of the food he was forced to survive on were equally frightening: Chicken heads floating in grease with a scattering of human fingernail clippings. The hooves of pigs, mules, and cows. A blackbird plopped on its back, feathers still on, feet facing upward and eyes shut tight.

The Hanoi Parade

Another POW right that the North Vietnamese freely violated concerned dignity and honor. Prisoners were to be protected against any "acts of violence or intimidation and against insults and public curiosity."

But like the North Koreans, the Viet Cong placed a high value on propaganda. They too were out to promote the cause of worldwide communism, which also meant making the United States look as bad as possible.

On July 6, 1966, fifty-two U.S. POWs took a long and wild walk among tens of thousands of angry Vietnamese people while reporters and camera crews from around the world looked on. This event being staged for the world press became known as the Hanoi Parade.

The blindfolded POWs had been collected from prisons in and around Hanoi. Guards made them assemble in a long column, two by two. Each pair stood ten feet behind the pair in front. With their inside hands cuffed together, the pairs could not break apart.

As they removed their blindfolds, an unreal scene unfolded in front of them. Stadium bleachers filled a wide traffic circle in downtown Hanoi. And sitting on those bleachers were thousands of people. What in the world were they all doing there? What were they waiting for?

The guards had the answers. It was them, the American POWs, that the crowd had come to see. Those thousands in the bleachers ahead hated the POWs so powerfully that they wished to kill them, the guards said. If the people acted on those wishes, their captors would do nothing to stop the violence.

Then the guards issued instructions. The twenty-six pairs of POWs were to walk in a line with their eyes straight ahead and their mouths shut tight along the entire two-mile route. As they marched, they were to show the thousands of Vietnamese people in front of them a proper attitude by bowing their heads in shame for all their crimes.

Outrages Upon Personal Dignity

The crowd kept an eerie silence as the parade of POWs approached. The fifty-two-man column was flanked by lines of guards. When the guards started shouting through bullhorns, the crowd suddenly came to life, shaking their fists and screaming at the prisoners.

A truck rolled alongside them carrying cameramen and reporters, mostly from European nations that were highly critical of the war, who kept calling to the POWs to keep their heads up so they could get a better look at them. At the same time, the guards yelled at them to keep their heads bowed in shame. The prisoners kept their heads up, not for the cameras but for their own dignity and self-respect.

Then people began breaking through the lines of guards to kick and punch the prisoners. From the people who could not get close enough there came a hail of stones, bottles, bricks, and garbage. The prisoners were bloody now, their clothes ripped and torn. The reporters and camera crews eagerly documented the spectacle.

Ahead, a stadium loomed: their destination. The POWs had to battle through the mob to reach it. Once they squeezed inside, the guards slammed the stadium doors shut behind them. Somehow all the POWs had made it there alive.

Twisted Facts

Then a public-address system crackled to life and a threatening voice had this to say: "You have seen the just wrath of the Vietnamese people. Those of you who have seen the light and want to apologize for your crimes and join the Vietnamese people will receive lenient and humane treatment."

What about those who had not seen the light? They would be turned over to the fury of the people outside.

When all the prisoners turned down this offer, they were herded back into the trucks that had brought them and returned to their prisons. Instead of suffering the fury of the crowd outside the Hanoi stadium, they had to endure furious beatings by the guards.

The prisoners had not cooperated by keeping their heads bowed and apologizing. But that did not stop the North Vietnamese from twisting the facts to turn the Hanoi Parade into a propaganda victory. Radio Hanoi's report proudly announced that, while some of the U.S. prisoners appeared arrogant at first, their attitudes changed when they were faced with "the wrath and protests of the population." At that point, "all of them marched docilely, their heads bent, their faces pale and sweating with fear."

Meanwhile, the report continued, the people of Hanoi, though "seething with anger at the crimes committed by the U.S. air pirates, showed themselves to be highly disciplined; otherwise the sheer thought of these crimes might have prompted them to tear [the prisoners] to pieces!"

Dark Secrets

An agreement to end U.S. participation in the Vietnam War was reached on January 23, 1973. As U.S. troops left Vietnam, 591 U.S. POWs were released.

But were those all the U.S. POWs in Vietnam? Or were the Viet Cong still holding on to some? These same kinds of questions were still being asked about U.S. POWs from the Korean War.

If the North Koreans and North Vietnamese had granted prisoners their basic rights, no one would have had to ask these questions. As called for in the 1949 Convention, the International Committee of the Red Cross should have been free to inspect POW camps, collect information about prisoners, and notify the country of origin of each prisoner's whereabouts and general condition.

But the Viet Cong, like the North Koreans, routinely refused to permit the Red Cross to inspect their camps or to furnish Red Cross representatives with the names of prisoners being held. The same violations were taking place in South Vietnamese POW prisons. Naturally, neither government wanted the world to know the dark details of these violations, but this was especially true of the Viet Cong. If details of their mistreatment of U.S. POWs became known, the Viet Cong could suffer a major propaganda setback.

The Tiger Cages

In the early 1970s, word got out that prisoners were being kept in solitary confinement and starved and tortured in POW prisons in both North and South Vietnam. But it was dramatic photographs of South Vietnamese political prisoners that caused the biggest single stir. Published in the July 17, 1970, issue of *Life* magazine, they showed the infamous "Tiger Cages of Con Son," hidden deep inside a huge South Vietnamese prison complex.

The photographs were taken by members of a committee sent to Vietnam by President Richard Nixon to investigate how prisoners were being treated. Two of the committee members were U.S. congressmen. They had with them a map that a former Tiger Cage prisoner had drawn. During their tour of the Con Son prison, they slipped away from their guides and found the cages. Thomas Harkin, a congressional aide, was with them,

**HERE IS ONE OF THE INFAMOUS "TIGER CAGES" ON CON SON ISLAND,
SIXTY MILES OFF THE SOUTH VIETNAMESE COAST. THE TINY CAGES
WERE USED TO CONFINE SOUTH VIETNAMESE POLITICAL PRISONERS
DURING THE VIETNAM WAR.**

and he took the pictures. Later, Harkin would become a
U.S. senator.

Each cage was a five-by-eight-foot stone room occupied by three to five prisoners. There were four hundred
prisoners in all. As many as three hundred were women.
Many appeared to be near death. Some begged for water.

These were not U.S. POWs. They were Vietnamese citizens held because the South Vietnamese government did
not approve of their political or religious beliefs. The photographs, along with stories of their inhumane treatment,
helped arouse anger and outrage for the war in general
and for what prisoners were suffering in particular.

73

Then there were the horrific stories told by the few U.S. POWs who had been released by the Viet Cong. And more horrific stories of what happened to Viet Cong POWs after U.S. soldiers turned them over to South Vietnamese police.

Millions of U.S. citizens signed petitions and wrote letters to government officials. They demanded that the torture on both sides stop, that camp conditions improve, and that Red Cross representatives be allowed into the camps. As a result, conditions for POWs in Vietnam may have improved somewhat during the last few years of the war, but neither government ended its policy of secrecy when it came to prisoners of war.

Cruel Consequences

After the return of 591 prisoners in the spring of 1973, more than 2,000 Americans were still listed as missing. But the U.S. government conducted investigations and announced that all living U.S. soldiers who had been POWs or who had been listed as missing in action (MIA) had been returned. The investigation included interviewing the repatriated prisoners, none of whom knew anything about any missing prisoners. As far as the government was concerned, the case of missing soldiers from the Vietnam War was closed.

But some of the families of soldiers listed as missing still wonder if their loved ones might be alive. Perhaps they are still being held prisoner somewhere in southeast Asia and could be rescued.

Now and again these families find tantalizing bits of evidence to keep them wondering. Since the war's end, there have been thousands of reports of American soldiers sighted in Vietnam—all unconfirmed. Satellite photos also have appeared, supposedly showing distress signals that missing American soldiers might have burned or stomped into fields—also unconfirmed.

The 1205 Document

Perhaps the most hopeful report came in 1993, when Harvard scholar Stephen Morris was rummaging through a room in Moscow, the Russian capital, where historical documents were stored. He found what appeared to be a translation, from Vietnamese into Russian, of a document written by a high-ranking official in the North Vietnamese Army.

It is known as the "1205 document" because it stated that a total of 1,205 American POWs were being held in North Vietnam as of September 1972. Subtract the 591 who were repatriated and that leaves 614 prisoners unaccounted for. The document also mentions an entirely separate system of North Vietnamese prisons that none of the 591 returned POWs could have known about.

Was this document genuine? Were its contents accurate? No one could say for sure. But independent experts who examined the 1205 document considered it authentic.

Totalitarianism and Torture

The Persian Gulf War, or Desert Storm, which began and ended in 1991, was fought over oil rights. Iraq, an Arab oil state, accused Kuwait, its neighbor and another Arab oil state, of illegally drilling for oil in Iraq's territory. On August 2, 1990, Iraq attacked Kuwait.

Five months later, United Nations coalition forces from thirty nations, led by the United States, intervened. They drove the invading Iraqi forces out of Kuwait, bringing the war to an abrupt end. Desert Storm lasted less than

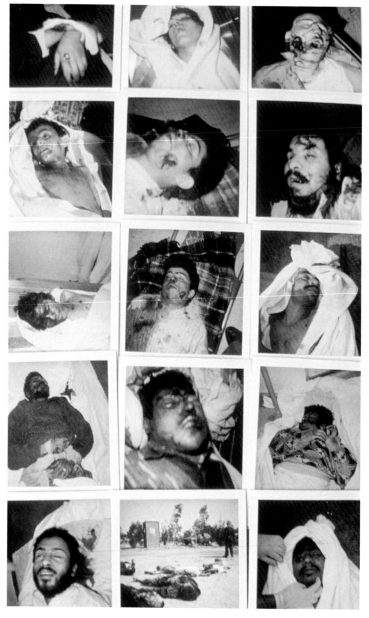

THESE PHOTOGRAPHS SHOW KUWAITI VICTIMS TORTURED BY IRAQI
FORCES DURING THE PERSIAN GULF WAR.

a year. Still, it was time enough to judge how well the two sides had honored the Geneva Conventions.

Iraq was a totalitarian society, a one-party government headed by iron-fisted ruler Saddam Hussein. A totalitarian dictator uses whatever methods he must to control all aspects of his citizens' lives. So it came as no surprise that Iraq violated the 1949 Convention article outlawing torture.

Seven U.S. airmen were shot down over Iraq during the fighting and captured by Iraqi soldiers. One of them was Air Force Major Jeffrey S. Tice. He used the word *hell* to describe the forty-five days he spent in Iraqi captivity. Tice lost twenty-nine pounds from lack of food while confined in a cell that measured six by nine feet. Bruises from beatings with hard rubber clubs covered his body. His teeth were chipped from grinding together as his ears and chin were wrapped with electrical wires.

Tice, along with the six other captured airmen, was forced to appear on Iraqi television broadcasts. This violated the 1949 Convention rule calling for prisoners to be protected "against acts of violence or intimidation and against insults and public curiosity."

A Cautious War

This was the first war involving United States troops since Vietnam, and that had been a highly unpopular war, stirring up protests all across the country. The U.S. military was concerned that this might happen again with Desert Storm. There was strong support for this war at home, and U.S. commanders were determined that there would be no violations of the Geneva Conventions from their troops to undermine this support.

So some two hundred military lawyers were sent to the Persian Gulf. Their job: to make sure that coalition forces treated civilians, combatants, and prisoners according to the laws and customs of war.

This careful and thoughtful approach contributed to the successful results. Coalition forces fought a winning war with little in the way of controversy to mar the result.

Like the other wars before it, looking all the way back to the Revolutionary War, the U.S. military had maintained high standards when it came to the treatment of enemy prisoners.

Those standards would be severely tested a decade later, though, when the United States would be forced to fight a new kind of war with a new and disturbing brand of enemy.

9
Unconventional Combatants

On September 11, 2001, the nature of warfare took a radical shift. Sixty years earlier, on December 7, 1941, Japan's air force all but destroyed the U.S. Pacific Fleet of seventeen warships in Pearl Harbor, Hawaii, prompting the United States to declare war on Japan and join in the fighting in World War II. That craftily coordinated sneak attack by hundreds of pilots in fighter planes and bombers was one of the defining moments of history.

So, too, was the September 11 surprise attack on the World Trade Center towers in New York City and the Pentagon in Washington, D.C. Again, the weapons were aircraft.

A Different Kind of Warfare

This time, instead of using military fighters and bombers made for warfare, the attackers hijacked commercial airliners carrying passengers. Instead of bombs, shells, and bullets, the weapons were the aircraft themselves. The men who hijacked them did not belong to an air force. They did

Al-Qaeda's Aims

The U.S. Department of Defense defines *terrorism* as "the unlawful use of—or threatened use of—force or violence against individuals or property to coerce or intimidate governments or societies, often to achieve political, religious, or ideological objectives." What were the 9/11 terrorists' objectives? What did they hope to achieve?

One of Al-Qaeda's immediate aims was to get Americans and all they stood for—including democracy—out of all Muslim nations, the nations in which the vast majority of people practice the Islamic faith. Such nations include Iraq, Iran, Saudi Arabia, Syria, Pakistan, Malaysia, and Indonesia. Al-Qaeda also hoped to overthrow the governments of Muslim nations such as Saudi Arabia and Kuwait, which were friendly toward the United States.

Then, said their elusive leader, Osama Bin Laden, who was thought to have masterminded the 9/11 attacks, all Muslims would unite to form a single country. And that vast Muslim nation of a billion-plus people would wage an all-out holy war against the United States and Israel.

not wear uniforms. They were not even licensed pilots. But their attack on the United States, like the Japanese attack sixty years earlier, was a shocking success.

The attack on Pearl Harbor was an act of traditional warfare. The 9/11 attack was a very different kind of violence, an act of asymmetric warfare. That's where one side has no hope of matching the other in terms of numbers and firepower. Instead, the weaker side finds ways to exploit chinks in the stronger side's armor, small weaknesses in an otherwise powerful opponent.

Asymmetric warfare is all about sneak attacks by the weak against the strong, designed to inspire fear and bring about political change. As in the 9/11 attacks, the victims are often noncombatants. Asymmetric warfare breaks the laws and customs of war. It is the warfare of terrorism.

A Different Kind of War

The U.S. Congress responded to the 9/11 attacks by passing an emergency resolution authorizing President George W. Bush to use all necessary force against those responsible for planning, aiding, or committing terrorist attacks or harboring those responsible for those attacks.

The nineteen hijackers who carried out the attack were traced to Al-Qaeda and the Taliban. To strike back, the president sent troops to Afghanistan to attack the Taliban. He also ordered U.S. Special Forces to various locations in the Middle East to hunt for Al-Qaeda leader Osama Bin Laden.

So began the "War on Terrorism." A formal declaration of war between nations was never issued. This would not be a war that could be won with one nation surrendering to another. This was a war against a terrorist ideology that knew no national boundaries, a conflict with no end in sight.

SEEKING INFORMATION
ALERT

These individuals are being sought in connection with possible terrorist threats against the United States.

AHMED KHALFAN GHAILANI

FAZUL ABDULLAH MOHAMMED

AMER EL-MAATI

AAFIA SIDDIQUI

ADAM YAHIYE GADAHN

ABDERRAOUF JDEY

ADNAN G. EL SHUKRIJUMAH

CONTACT INFORMATION

IF YOU HAVE ANY INFORMATION CONCERNING THESE INDIVIDUALS, PLEASE CONTACT THE LOCAL FBI OFFICE OR THE NEAREST AMERICAN EMBASSY OR CONSULATE.

THIS FBI WANTED POSTER, RELEASED IN 2004, SHOWS SEVEN PEOPLE SUSPECTED OF INVOLVEMENT IN TERRORIST ACTIVITIES WITHIN THE UNITED STATES.

POWs Defined

It was also a war between conventional and unconventional combatants, a fact that raised questions about prisoners of war. War is combat, the act of fighting. Before their capture, nearly all prisoners of war were combatants: soldiers, sailors, airmen, or marines involved in armed conflict. This definition rules out ordinary civilians. Being noncombatants, they cannot become POWs.

Article 4 of the 1949 Convention on POWs defines combatants as fitting into certain categories. They include "[m]embers of the armed forces of a Party to the conflict, as well as militias or volunteer corps forming part of such armed forces." To these categories the article adds members of "organized resistance movements." But to qualify for POW status, combatants in these categories must fulfill the following conditions:

(a) that of being commanded by a person responsible for his subordinates;

(b) that of having a fixed distinctive sign [such as a uniform] recognizable at a distance;

(c) that of carrying arms openly;

(d) that of conducting their operations in accordance with the laws and customs of war.

To the categories of combatants who qualify for POW status, Article 4 also adds members of organized resistance movements fighting against enemy forces occupying their nations, as well as

[I]nhabitants of a non-occupied territory, who on the approach of the enemy spontaneously take up

arms to resist the invading forces, without having had time to form themselves into regular armed units, provided they carry arms openly and respect the laws and customs of war.

Unconventional But Not Unprotected

As to combatants who do not fit any of these categories, Article 5 of the 1949 POW Convention says: "Should any doubt arise as to whether [captured combatants] belong to any of the categories enumerated in Article 4, such persons shall enjoy the protection of the present Convention until . . . their status has been determined by a competent tribunal."

That is, some captured combatants may not meet all four conditions noted above. These unconventional combatants may not be in uniform, for example, or they may be accused of deliberately targeting civilians, as in the case of terrorists. Even then, they must be treated as prisoners of war until a military court rules on their status.

And what happens when a court rules that captured combatants are not entitled to POW status? Such persons are still protected under the provisions of the Fourth Geneva Convention Relative to the Protection of Civilian Persons in Time of War. According to international law, there is no such thing as an unprotected person in time of war. Even captured terrorists are protected by the Fourth Convention and must be treated fairly and humanely.

A New Set of Rules

In December 2001, Defense Secretary Donald Rumsfeld announced that prisoners in the War on Terrorism would be moved from Afghanistan to a detainment camp at the Guantanamo Bay U.S. Naval Base, Cuba. The base came to the United States in a 1903 agreement with the newly formed government of the Republic of Cuba. That was after U.S. troops helped Cuba gain its independence from Spain. The base remains in U.S. control as long as the United States chooses to hold on to it.

Prisoners began arriving in January 2002. By April they were all being held in a prison within Guantanamo called Camp Delta. Cells were arranged in blocks, twenty-four cells to a block. Each cell had a sink with running water, a flush toilet, and an elevated metal bed frame. Cells were made of metal mesh and measured 8 feet long, 6 feet 8 inches wide, and 8 feet tall. Some were exposed to the sun, others were in the shade.

These accommodations would appear to violate the 1949 POW Convention, which states:

> **Prisoners of war shall be quartered under conditions as favorable as those for the forces of the Detaining Power who are billeted in the same area. . . . The foregoing provisions shall apply in particular to the dormitories of prisoners of war as regards both total surface and minimum cubic space, and the general installations, bedding and blankets.**

U.S. troops quartered at the base to run the prison were not living like this, out in the open in cramped mesh cells.

Unlawful Combatants

The Bush administration saw things differently. In January 2002, Secretary of Defense Rumsfeld issued a memo to all combat commanders ordering that "Al-Qaeda and Taliban individuals . . . are not entitled to prisoner of war status for purposes of the Geneva Conventions of 1949."

THE HOODED MAN IS SUSPECTED OF BEING A MEMBER OF THE TALIBAN, OR AL-QAEDA, IN AFGHANISTAN. HE HAS BEEN TAKEN INTO CUSTODY BY A U.S. MILITARY POLICE OFFICER. THE PHOTO WAS TAKEN ON JUNE 2, 2003.

Why not? Because, said the administration, these men were unlawful combatants. They did not observe the laws and rules of war. They did not belong to an armed force with a clear command structure. They did not wear uniforms or carry weapons openly, and they deliberately targeted civilians.

The administration did not comment on the passage in Article 5 about military courts or the Convention's insistence that in time of war, there is no such thing as an unprotected person. However, the memo went on to say, commanders should "treat [Al Qaeda and Taliban prisoners] humanely, and *to the extent appropriate and consistent with military necessity*, consistent with the Geneva Conventions of 1949." (Italics added.)

At first glance, the administration's statement appears to say that although these prisoners do not qualify as POWs, they should be treated humanely just the same. But the phrase "to the extent appropriate and consistent with military necessity" is meant to allow for wide exceptions. The International Law of War Association (ILOWA) is a human rights group composed of legal professionals. In its opinion, "That order thus gives commanders permission to depart, where they deem it appropriate and a military necessity, from the provisions of the Geneva Conventions."

A New Paradigm

In a memo of January 25, 2002, White House Counsel Alberto Gonzales agreed:

> **The nature of [a war against terrorism] places a high premium on . . . the ability to quickly obtain information from captured terrorists and their sponsors in order to avoid further atrocities**

against American civilians. . . . [T]his new paradigm
renders obsolete Geneva's strict limitations on
questioning of enemy prisoners.

By "strict limitations on questioning," Gonzales
appears to refer to this sentence from Article 17 of the
1949 POW Convention: "No physical or mental torture,
nor any other form of coercion, may be inflicted on
prisoners of war to secure from them information of any
kind whatever."

By "new paradigm," Gonzales means a new strategy
for fighting this new kind of war, including new interrogation techniques for prisoners. According to journalist Jane
Mayer, writing in the *New Yorker* magazine, this new
strategy for conducting the war on terrorism rests on the
belief that "the President, as Commander-in-Chief, has
the authority to disregard virtually all previously known
legal boundaries, if national security demands it."

The Bush Order

On February 7, 2002, President Bush turned the sugges-
tions in these memos into law with an order that labeled
Taliban and Al-Qaeda captives not prisoners of war but
"unlawful combatants." Later he amended the order.
The 1949 Convention would now apply to Taliban—but
not Al-Qaeda—captives. However, the amended order
added, Taliban captives would not be considered true prisoners of war, and so they would not necessarily be granted
all POW rights.

What was wrong with granting the Taliban captives
unconditional POW status? Because then, as stated in
the POW Convention, military interrogators could right-
fully demand only that a Taliban prisoner give his or her
name, rank, date of birth, and serial number. After that the
prisoner could refuse to answer any further questions,

confident that he or she would not be coerced with inhumane treatment.

To further complicate matters, the Bush administration argued, the 1949 Convention did not adequately define the terms *inhumane, coercion,* and *outrages upon personal dignity*. This would make it hard on interrogators whose job it was to obtain vital information from captives in the War on Terrorism. They could never be sure how far they were allowed to go in trying to get this information.

A Never-Ending War

Then there was the matter of repatriation. Article 118 of the 1949 Convention states that prisoners of war must be "repatriated without delay after the cessation of active hostilities." So, if the captives were granted full POW rights, they would have to be sent back to their home countries one day, provided that the War on Terrorism ever came to an end.

These individuals were very different from captives taken in previous wars, the administration argued. When a traditional war ends, the fighters lay down their weapons and go home. Even if they wanted to go on fighting, they couldn't, not without an organized army in which to fight. The vast majority of these former soldiers were glad the war was over. They welcomed peace. In time they would have a change of heart, and all the bad feelings toward their former enemy would fade away.

But these Taliban and Al-Qaeda captives were a different breed. They did not fight in a national army. They did not welcome peace. For terrorists, the war would never end. For them it was a *jihad,* a holy war against infidels: people who, since they do not believe in the same god, would always be the enemy. And that was why the administration saw Taliban and Al-Qaeda prisoners as unlawful combatants who deserved indefinite imprisonment.

War Crimes

Finally, the Bush administration was concerned about the issue of war crimes. The Geneva Conventions defined war crimes as grave breaches, or serious violations, of the Conventions' laws. War crimes were also addressed in U.S. law. In his memo of January 25, 2002, White House Counsel Alberto Gonzales called attention to the 1996 War Crimes Act, a federal statute that bans Americans from committing war crimes.

The statute, which was expanded in 1997, calls for a possible death penalty punishment for those responsible if detainees should die from abusive treatment while in U.S. custody. Gonzales noted that the statute specifically applies to U.S. officials, from the president himself on down. Gonzales wrote, "It is difficult to predict the motives of prosecutors and independent counsels who may in the future decide to pursue unwarranted charges based on [the War Crimes Act]."

Therefore, the closer the United States agreed to stick to the 1949 Convention rights of captives in the War on Terrorism, the greater the danger that Bush administration members might one day find themselves on trial for war crimes. Therefore, Gonzales concluded, denying unconditional prisoner-of-war status to Taliban and Al Qaeda captives "substantially reduces the threat of domestic criminal prosecution under the War Crimes Act."

Powell Disagrees

Not everyone in the Bush administration agreed that the Guantanamo captives should be denied full prisoner of war rights. In his memo of January 25, 2002, White House Counsel Gonzales brought up the concerns of Secretary of State Colin Powell.

Powell was a military man. He had risen to the rank of

general in the U.S. Army. Perhaps that was why he saw things from a different point of view than other members of the administration. In the past, the United States had consistently followed the 1949 POW Convention when it came to the treatment of prisoners of war, Powell pointed out, even though some other nations had not.

Now, to abruptly abandon the Convention "will reverse over a century of U.S. policy and practice in supporting the Geneva conventions and undermine the protections of the law of war for our troops, both in this specific conflict and in general," Powell wrote in a memo to Gonzales.

Powell added that not following the convention would also have serious consequences in terms of reciprocity:

- **It has a high cost in terms of negative international reaction, with immediate adverse consequences for our conduct of foreign policy.**

- **It will undermine public support among critical allies, making military cooperation more difficult to sustain.**

- **Europeans and others will likely have legal problems with extradition or other forms of cooperation in law enforcement, including in bringing terrorists to justice.**

Despite Powell's objections, the administration stuck to its decision. The Guantanamo captives would not be considered prisoners of war and need not be treated as such.

Human Rights Groups Protest

The Bush Order was sharply criticized by human rights groups, who saw it as a clear violation of international law. Darcy Christen, spokesperson for the International Committee of the Red Cross, said flatly: "They were captured in combat [and] we consider them prisoners of war."

Christen also pointed to Article 5 of the 1949 Convention, which states that if there is any doubt about whether captives should be considered prisoners of war, "such persons shall enjoy the protection of the present Convention until such time as their status has been determined by a competent tribunal."

Christen added, "You cannot simply decide . . . what applies to one person and what applies to another. This has to go to court because it is a legal decision, not a political one." And no court had been held to determine the status of any Taliban or Al-Qaeda captive.

Legal Rights Denied

The 1949 Convention was not the only international law agreement that concerned these captives' status. A resolution adopted by the United Nations General Assembly in 1988, known as Body of Principles for the Protection of All Persons under Any Form of Detention or Imprisonment, also applied.

The agreement consists of thirty-nine principles. These two are particularly important to prisoner-of-war rights:

Principle 10
Anyone who is arrested shall be informed at the time of his arrest of the reason for his arrest and shall be promptly informed of any charges against him.

Principle 11
1. A person shall not be kept in detention without being given an effective opportunity to be heard

promptly by a judicial or other authority. A detained person shall have the right to defend himself or to be assisted by counsel as prescribed by law.

2. A detained person and his counsel, if any, shall receive prompt and full communication of any order of detention, together with the reasons therefore.

3. A judicial or other authority shall be empowered to review as appropriate the continuance of detention.

The Taliban and Al-Qaeda captives did not enjoy the rights listed in these principles. What were the charges against them? What was the evidence against them? No one would say. Until someone did tell them why they were being held, they had no hope of defending themselves in any court of law. Meanwhile, their captors could, if they wished, detain them at Guantanamo indefinitely.

10
Prisoners Outside the Law

The Center for Constitutional Rights (CCR) is an organization of legal professionals whose mission is "to guarantee the rights of those with the fewest protections and least access to legal resources." In February 2002, the CCR filed a petition in federal court on behalf of several Guantanamo detainees.

The petition cited these facts: The detainees had never been charged with crimes. They had not been allowed to see lawyers. They were unable to bring their cases to any sort of court. Yet they had been held captive for more than eighteen months.

Habeas Corpus

The CCR petition was a writ of habeas corpus. This is a Latin term meaning, literally, "you have the body."

"The body" in this case was the Guantanamo prisoners named in the petition. U.S. law prohibits authorities from holding a prisoner indefinitely without charging him or her with a crime. A *writ* is an order meant to force the authorities to either charge a suspect with a crime or release him or her.

International law specifically supports habeas corpus. The 1949 Convention calls for the Detaining Power to specify (1) "the charge or charges on which the prisoner of war is to be arraigned" and (2) "the court which will try the case, likewise the date and place fixed for the opening of the trial." The convention also states: "Judicial investigations relating to a prisoner of war shall be conducted as rapidly as circumstances permit."

The writ of habeas corpus, if granted, guarantees two things. First, a court will review the prisoner's case and decide whether his or her confinement is legal. Second, if the court rules that there is no lawful basis for holding the prisoner, he or she will be released. This is what the petitioners for the Guantanamo detainees were asking: that the prisoners either be charged with a crime or set free.

No-Man's-Land

However, the Bush administration had placed the Guantanamo captives into a kind of legal no-man's-land. They were not prisoners of war protected by the 1949 Convention and other treaties of international law, the administration declared, but they also were not criminal suspects protected by the U.S. Constitution.

Why not? Because the Guantanamo Bay Naval Base was not actually a part of the United States of America. It too was a kind of legal no-man's-land.

And so, according to the Bush administration, the Guantanamo captives were left stranded outside the law. They had no legal rights of any kind. In the past, the ICRC had reviewed similar situations and had come to different conclusions:

> **Every person in enemy hands must have some status under international law: he is either a prisoner of war and, as such, covered by the Third**

The Right to Liberty and Security

Habeas corpus, a speedy trial, and other judicial rights show up repeatedly in international human rights documents. Those listed below are from a treaty called the United Nations International Covenant on Civil and Political Rights, entered into force in 1976.

1. Everyone has the right to liberty and security of person. No one shall be subjected to arbitrary arrest or detention. No one shall be deprived of his liberty except on such grounds and in accordance with such procedures as are established by law.

2. Anyone who is arrested shall be informed, at the time of arrest, of the reasons for his arrest and shall be promptly informed of any charges against him.

3. Anyone arrested or detained on a criminal charge shall be brought promptly before a judge or other officer authorized by law to exercise judicial power and shall be entitled to trial within a reasonable time or

to release. It shall not be the general rule that persons awaiting trial shall be detained in custody, but release may be subject to guarantees to appear for trial, at any other stage of the judicial proceedings, and, should occasion arise, for execution of the judgment.

4. Anyone who is deprived of his liberty by arrest or detention shall be entitled to take proceedings before a court, in order that court may decide without delay on the lawfulness of his detention and order his release if the detention is not lawful.

5. Anyone who has been the victim of unlawful arrest or detention shall have an enforceable right to compensation.

The United States, along with most of the world's nations, has ratified the covenant.

> Convention, a civilian covered by the Fourth Con-
> vention, [or] a member of the medical personnel of
> the armed forces who is covered by the First Con-
> vention. There is no intermediate status; nobody in
> enemy hands can fall outside the law.

Winston Churchill also had weighed in on these issues. Churchill was prime minister of Great Britain during World War II and worked with President Roosevelt on the Atlantic Charter. He had said:

> The power of the Executive to cast a man into
> prison without formulating any charge known to
> the law, and particularly to deny him the judgment
> of his peers, is in the highest degree odious and is
> the foundation of all totalitarian government
> whether Nazi or Communist. . . . Extraordinary
> power assumed by the Executive should be yielded
> up when the emergency declines. Nothing is more
> abhorrent than to imprison a person or keep him in
> prison because he is unpopular. This is really the
> test of civilization.

The Lower Courts Decide

What did the U.S. courts think of the habeas corpus petition for the Guantanamo detainees, which was named *Rasul, et al., v. Bush, President of the United States, et al.*? In August 2002, the U.S. District Court dismissed the petition. The court's ruling agreed with the Bush administration's reasoning: The district court could not honor this habeas petition because the Guantanamo detainees were not U.S. citizens and they were not being detained inside U.S. borders.

The CCR then took the next step up the judicial ladder and petitioned the U.S. Court of Appeals. This petition asked the court of appeals to reexamine the Bush adminis-

THIS PHOTO SHOWS SHAFIQ RASUL, A BRITISH CITIZEN HELD AT THE U.S. GUANTANAMO BAY PRISON CAMP. RASUL WAS TAKEN PRISONER IN 2002 AND RELEASED IN 2004. HE WAS AT THE CENTER OF THE *RASUL V. BUSH* CASE.

tration's reasoning and reverse the district court ruling. But the court of appeals decided to let the ruling stand.

So the CCR took the case to the highest court in the land, the U.S. Supreme Court. In June 2004, the Supreme Court handed down its ruling in the matter of *Rasul* v. *Bush*. In a 6 to 3 vote, it reversed the court of appeals ruling. In doing so, the Supreme Court labeled the Bush administration's handling of the detainees "unconstitutional." It said the Guantanamo detainees did have the right to challenge their detention by filing writs of habeas corpus in U.S. courts. They also had the right to work with a lawyer to prepare a habeas petition.

The Supreme Court Decision

The Court's majority opinion in *Rasul* v. *Bush* was written by Justice John Paul Stevens. It summarized the detainees' situation this way: "They are not nationals of countries at war with the United States, and they deny that they have engaged in or plotted acts of aggression against this country; they have never been afforded access to any tribunal, much less charged with and convicted of wrongdoing. "

The Court's opinion had this to say about the legal status of the Guantanamo Bay Naval Base: "[A]nd for more than two years they have been imprisoned in territory over which the United States exercises exclusive jurisdiction and control." And so, with these words, the Court rejected two key Bush administration assertions: that the base was not U.S. territory and that the detainees were not under the jurisdiction of U.S. courts.

Then there was the fact that the detainees were not U.S. citizens. Did that mean they could be denied basic legal rights? The Court said no, it did not. U.S. courts have traditionally been open to nonresident aliens such as the Guantanamo detainees, who deserve the same legal rights as any U.S. citizen. The fact that these men were detained for more than two years without charge and without access to counsel "unquestionably describes custody in violation of the Constitution, laws or treaties of the United States," Justice Stevens wrote.

The High Court's ruling in *Rasul* v. *Bush* did not lay these issues to rest, however. In the years to come, the battle over the rights of the Guantanamo prisoners would continue. Meanwhile, another prisoner issue was stirring up even more controversy.

11
Prisoners and Torture

Detaining prisoners indefinitely is one thing; subjecting them to torture is another. No other issue in the War on Terrorism has incited such strong feelings and heated debate. The United Nations Convention Against Torture (CAT), passed in 1985, defines *torture* as:

> **any act by which severe pain or suffering, whether physical or mental, is intentionally inflicted on a person for such purposes as obtaining from him or a third person a confession, punishing him for an act he or a third person has committed or is suspected of having committed, or intimidating or coercing him or a third person . . . when such pain or suffering is inflicted by or at the instigation of or with the consent or acquiescence of a public official or other person acting in an official capacity.**

Torture Outlawed

The CAT does more than give torture a definition. It requires all states to outlaw and prevent torture at all times, including in time of war. "[N]o state of emergency, other external threats, nor orders from a superior officer or authority may be invoked to justify torture," it declares. The CAT also forbids countries to "export" prisoners for torture, to send them away to other countries "if there is reason to believe he/she will be tortured" in those countries.

By ratifying the CAT in 1994, the United States agreed to meet these requirements. Of course, the United States also ratified the 1949 Convention, which states that "murder of all kinds, mutilation, cruel treatment and torture . . . are and shall remain prohibited at any time and in any place whatsoever. . . ." And this prohibition applies to all detainees, even unlawful combatants.

The U.S. Army also set strict rules regarding torture. The Army's Field Manual 34–52, titled "Intelligence Interrogation," strictly forbids certain interrogation techniques that could be seen as torture. They include using chemicals to cause pain, depriving the prisoner of food, and forcing him to stand, sit, or kneel in abnormal positions for long periods of time. The manual also prohibits techniques used to cause mental pain, such as sleep deprivation and mock executions, where the prisoner is led to believe that his captors are about to kill him.

But then came the events of September 11, 2001. With them came the Bush administration's new paradigm, which, according to White House Counsel Gonzales, "renders obsolete Geneva's strict limitations on questioning of enemy prisoners."

Torture Redefined

The Bush administration saw the U.N. definition of torture—"severe pain and suffering, whether physical or mental"—as too general and limiting for the tough new War on Terrorism. Under the new paradigm, interrogators dealing with terrorist prisoners had to be freer to act.

That's why, in an August 2002 memo to the White House, the Justice Department proposed a much narrower definition of torture. An interrogator should be free to use painful techniques to get information from a prisoner. Only when those techniques brought too much pain should they be outlawed.

How much pain was too much? The techniques "must penetrate to the core of an individual's ability to perceive the world around him, substantially interfering with his cognitive abilities, or fundamentally alter his personality." Only when these techniques brought the prisoner as much pain as he would feel while his organs were failing and he was dying should they be considered torture, the Justice Department memo suggested.

The memo also proposed that interrogators who used torture under certain circumstances should be excused from blame. Torture should be considered illegal only if it could be proved that the interrogator intended to cause that much pain. And if the interrogator used torture because of some extraordinary military necessity, the torture might be acceptable. For example, if it was being done "in order to prevent further attacks on the United States by the Al-Qaeda terrorist network."

Abu Ghraib

In March 2003 the United States invaded Iraq, overthrew Saddam Hussein's dictatorship, and occupied the nation. Later, rebel forces of Islamic insurgents kept U.S. troops engaged in an ongoing war. In the process, U.S. troops put hundreds of captured insurgents into POW prisons inside Iraq. One of these prisons was Abu Ghraib, also known as Baghdad Correctional Facility, which held between 6,000 and 7,000 prisoners.

Inside Guantanamo

On the floor of the U.S. Senate, Senator Dick Durbin of Illinois read from an FBI agent's report describing what the agent witnessed inside the Guantanamo Bay prison:

> On a couple of occasions, I entered interview rooms to find a detainee chained hand and foot in a fetal position to the floor, with no chair, food or water. . . . On one occasion, the air conditioning had been turned down so far and the temperature was so cold in the room, that the barefooted detainee was shaking with cold. . . . On another occasion, the [air conditioner] had been turned off, making the temperature in the unventilated room well over 100 degrees. The detainee was almost unconscious on the floor, with a pile of hair next to him. He had apparently been literally pulling his hair out throughout the night. On another occasion, not only was the temperature unbearably hot, but extremely loud rap music was being played in the room, and had been since the day before, with the detainee chained hand and foot in the fetal position on the tile floor.

In April 2004, disturbing photographs taken within Abu Ghraib began showing up in newspapers, on television, and over the Internet. They showed U.S. soldiers who were serving as prison guards blatantly violating Article 14 of the 1949 Convention: "Prisoners of war are entitled in all circumstances to respect for their persons and their honor."

As they were being photographed, some prisoners were made to stand on boxes and chairs with hoods or underpants over their heads. Some were bound up naked and

THIS PHOTO, FIRST PUBLISHED IN THE *WASHINGTON POST*, SHOWS U.S. SOLDIER LYNNDIE ENGLAND HOLDING A LEASH TIED TO THE NECK OF A NAKED DETAINEE AT ABU GHRAIB PRISON. SHE WAS TRIED FOR ABUSE OF PRISONERS AND SENTENCED TO THREE YEARS BEHIND BARS.

arranged in groups or piled up. Some were being threat-ened by snarling dogs held on leashes by soldiers. One prisoner was being treated as if he were a dog himself, ly-ing on the floor at the end of a leash held by a female guard. Many of the prisoners in these photos appear to be injured, with blood coming from open wounds.

In two of the photos, a female soldier and a male sol-dier pose over the body of a prisoner named Manadel al-Jamadi. Both U.S. soldiers are looking up at the camera grinning. Jamadi's eyes are taped shut. He had died while being interrogated. According to doctors who examined his body, Manadel al-Jamadi had died of asphyxiation.

The Taguba Report

In May 2004 the U.S. military issued a report of an investi-gation into the Abu Ghraib abuses. The head investigator was Major General Antonio Taguba. The Taguba Report held prison guards responsible for the illegal abuse of detainees. It concluded that soldiers had "committed egregious acts and grave breaches of international law at Abu Ghraib."

The report listed both physical and psychological abuses, such as "punching, slapping, and kicking de-tainees"; "forcing naked male detainees to wear women's underwear"; "arranging naked male detainees in a pile and then jumping on them"; and "taking photographs of dead Iraqi detainees."

The Bush administration blamed these abuses on a few rogue soldiers. In 2005, seven soldiers were convicted in court-martials and sentenced to time in federal prison for their abuses of prisoners at Abu Ghraib. They were also dishonorably discharged from the Army. The commanding officer at the prison, Brigadier General Janis Karpinski, was demoted to the rank of colonel.

The Mikolashek Report

The Army's inspector general, Lieutenant General Paul Mikolashek, conducted another investigation. This one looked at reports of abuses to prisoners held by U.S. forces at sixteen prisons in Iraq and Afghanistan. The report blamed twenty detainee deaths and seventy-four other reported abuses on "the failure of individuals to follow known standards of discipline and Army values and, in some cases, the failure of a few leaders to enforce those standards of discipline."

However, the abuse cases involved only a tiny percentage of the more than 50,000 detainees held by U.S. forces in Iraq and Afghanistan, the report emphasized. "These abuses should be viewed as what they are—unauthorized actions taken by a few individuals."

Critics reacted to the reports. They singled out the Bush order denying Taliban and Al-Qaeda captives full and unconditional POW rights. Critics also pointed to the 2002 Gonzales memo on narrowing the definition of torture and relaxing restrictions on interrogation techniques. They claimed that these policy decisions laid the groundwork for the interrogation abuses, including the deaths, at Abu Ghraib and elsewhere.

Ghost Detainees

In 2004 the *Washington Post* newspaper revealed another aspect of the U.S. War on Terrorism prisoner program. The key agency in the *Post* articles was the Central Intelligence Agency (CIA), which is responsible for conducting espionage operations outside U.S. borders.

The *Post* had learned that the CIA ran a string of secret jails in nations outside the United States, including Thailand, Iraq, Afghanistan, and Qatar. Abu Ghraib was one of these "black sites," as the CIA calls them.

Before the *Post* articles, the existence of these secret jails for the War on Terrorism was known to only a few government officials, including the president, outside of the CIA. By exporting terrorist suspects to these facilities for safekeeping and interrogation, the CIA could keep them out of the public eye. These "ghost detainees," as they were sometimes known, had no legal rights. They could not consult a lawyer or have their cases brought before any kind of court.

Holding prisoners in isolation in secret prisons in the United States is illegal. That was one reason the CIA exported these prisoners overseas. In July 2006, the United Nations reacted to this practice. The UN Human Rights Committee said that the United States should shut down all the secret prisons it used in the War on Terrorism. The United States "should only detain persons in places in which they can enjoy the full protection of the law," the committee declared.

The CIA would not comment on these black sites. The agency would not even admit publicly that they existed. But some former CIA members talked with the media about them. The *Post* quoted former CIA officer Peter Probst: "People tend to regard [taking prisoners to black sites] as an extra-judicial kidnapping; it's not. There is a long history of this. It has been done for decades. It's absolutely legal."

Enhanced Techniques

At these secret sites, CIA agents can interrogate terrorist suspects without fear of interference from courts, human rights groups, or U.S. military officials who might not approve of their interrogation methods. Agents can use their own set of rules to determine how they will interrogate suspected terrorists.

The CIA developed these rules after the September

11, 2001, attacks. CIA officials have testified before Congress that they do not use torture during their interrogations. But they sometimes use what they refer to as "enhanced interrogation techniques," which may cause temporary physical or mental pain. CIA rules call for agents in these secret jails to first get approval from Washington before using any of these techniques.

There are six of them. In the "Attention Grab," the interrogator grabs the prisoner by the shirt front and shakes him. In the "Attention Slap," the interrogator delivers a slap with his open hand that is meant to cause pain and bring fear.

The "Belly Slap" is a hard open-handed slap to the stomach. The aim is to cause pain but not any long-lasting internal damage. The "Long Time Standing" technique keeps the prisoner standing handcuffed and with his feet shackled to the floor for forty hours and more. The resulting extreme exhaustion and lack of sleep sometimes leads to a confession.

In the "Cold Cell," the prisoner must stand stark naked in a cell with the temperature at fifty degrees. As he stands there, he is doused with cold water. Finally, in "Waterboarding," the subject is made to believe that he is drowning.

Extreme Rendition

Other groups of prisoners are transported to other nations around the world by the CIA and other U.S. government agencies. The prisoners are turned over to those nations' intelligence services for interrogation. These host nations include Syria, Morocco, Jordan, Egypt, and Saudi Arabia. All are frequently cited by the United Nations and by human rights groups for human rights violations, including torture.

Waterboarding

None of the CIA's enhanced interrogation techniques is more controversial than waterboarding. This extreme technique of persuasion probably originated in the Middle Ages. Back then, the victim was strapped to a board and tilted back into a body of water headfirst, left that way for a few seconds, then pulled out to get a breath. The process was repeated until the victim cooperated with his captors.

In the modern version of waterboarding, a piece of plastic wrap is added. Captors place it over the victim's face. Then, after tilting the board so that the victim's head is lower than his feet, they pour a stream of water onto the plastic wrap. In a matter of seconds the victim feels as if he is at death's door, on the verge of drowning.

CIA officers say it takes about fourteen seconds for the average person to cave in and give up after waterboarding. Who lasted longest? Al-Qaeda's Khalid Sheikh Mohammed, said to be the principal architect of the 9/11 attacks, lasted more than two minutes before he gave up and confessed.

Human rights advocates point to waterboarding as a particularly extreme form of interrogation. John Sifton of Human Rights Watch says that "it really amounts to a mock execution, which is illegal under international law." Waterboarding is also prohibited by U.S. military law.

Shipping prisoners to these other nations for harsh questioning is known as extreme rendition. CIA officers masked and dressed in black often carry out these actions. They dress their captives in black and blindfold them before carrying them away and sending them off to the host nations for interrogation.

Extreme rendition keeps the CIA at a distance from what goes on during interrogation of these prisoners. If inhumane techniques are used to gain information, CIA interrogators cannot be held directly responsible, since the abuse took place far away from them in another country.

The Arar Case

A victim of extreme rendition was Maher Arar, a Canadian citizen of Syrian descent living in British Columbia. Arar was observed by Canadian authorities talking with two other Muslim Canadians who were suspected of having links to Al-Qaeda. Canada warned U.S. immigration authorities, who had Arar arrested at a New York airport in September 2002 and held for questioning.

Arar insisted that the men were only casual acquaintances, but U.S. authorities had him secretly flown to Jordan and then driven to neighboring Syria, a nation with a longstanding reputation for serious human rights abuses. There, Arar was kept in a dungeon the size of a coffin and interrogated for ten months. The interrogations included regular beating. Finally, he was freed as a result of persistent pressure from the Canadian government.

A special Canadian commission investigated Arar's renditioning. It concluded that he had been falsely accused, that there was no evidence to indicate that Arar had done anything wrong or posed any kind of threat. In a *Washington Post* interview, commission member Paul Cavalluzzo said that "an innocent Canadian was tortured, his life was put upside down, and it set him back years and years."

Tortured Confessions

While the Arar interrogations were carried out by Syrians, interrogations carried out by CIA agents also have come under harsh criticism, some of it from officials in the U.S. intelligence community itself. In 2004, CIA inspector general John Helgerwon issued a report stating that the CIA's so-called enhanced interrogation techniques "appeared to constitute cruel and degrading treatment under the [Geneva] Convention."

Former CIA officer Bob Baer labeled these same techniques bad interrogation. "I mean you can get anyone to confess to anything if the torture's bad enough," he said.

Former FBI agent Dan Coleman agreed. In a news interview, he expressed his anger at lawyers in Washington who helped write the new CIA War on Terrorism interrogation rules. Coleman asked, "Have any of these guys ever tried to talk to someone who's been deprived of his clothes?" Coleman answered his own question: "He's going to be ashamed, and humiliated, and cold. He'll tell you anything you want to hear to get his clothes back. There's no value in it."

Bush on Torture

How did the Bush administration feel about using torture to interrogate prisoners in the War on Terrorism? Time and again in their public statements, the president and members of his administration have expressed vehement opposition to the use of torture under any circumstances. In February 2002, Mr. Bush said, "Of course our values as a nation . . . call for us to treat detainees humanely, including those who are not legally entitled to such treatment."

In September 2003, the president issued a statement declaring: "Torture anywhere is an affront to human dignity everywhere. . . . Freedom from torture is an inalienable human right. . . . The United States is committed to the world-wide elimination of torture and we are leading this fight by example. I call on all governments to join with the United States and the community of law-abiding nations in prohibiting, investigating, and prosecuting all acts of torture and in undertaking to prevent other cruel and unusual punishment."

In June 2004, he said, "Let me make very clear the position of my government and our country. We do not condone torture. I have never ordered torture. I will never order torture. The values of this country are such that torture is not a part of our soul and our being."

And in a January 2005 interview with the *New York Times*, Bush stated flatly that "torture is never acceptable, nor do we hand over people to countries that do torture."

In May 2006, representatives of the Bush administration spoke before the United Nations Committee Against Torture. John B. Bellinger, a U.S. State Department adviser, insisted that the abuses at Abu Ghraib were isolated incidents. The United States continues to be dedicated to eradicating torture everywhere in the world, he said.

12
A Matter of Honor

Some legislators thought the Bush administration's anti-torture statements were not enough. They were responding to the worldwide media exposure of prisoner abuse at Abu Ghraib, Guantanamo Bay, and other U.S. detention facilities around the world that contradicted the administration's publicly stated opposition to torture. These lawmakers wanted Congress to show the world in no uncertain terms that Americans did not condone the use of torture in dealing with prisoners of war and would not use torture in the future.

One such lawmaker was former Vietnam POW John McCain, who had been a U.S. senator from Arizona since 1985. On October 5, 2005, McCain proposed a new law that would establish the U.S. Army Field Manual on Interrogation as the uniform standard for the interrogation of Department of Defense detainees. It would also prohibit cruel, inhumane, and degrading treatment of prisoners being held by the government.

Legally and Morally Wrong

What does the U.S. Army tell soldiers about questioning prisoners of war? *Army Field Manual 34–52*, chapter 1, sets forth the basic principles of interrogation. A key section titled "Prohibition Against Use of Force" begins this way: "The use of force, mental torture, threats, insults, or exposure to unpleasant and inhumane treatment of any kind is prohibited by law and is neither authorized nor condoned by the US Government."

The manual goes on to say that "the use of force is not necessary to gain the cooperation of sources for interrogation." Why? Because force "yields unreliable results . . . and can induce the source to say whatever he thinks the interrogator wants to hear."

The manual allows interrogators to use "psychological ploys, verbal trickery, or other nonviolent and noncoercive ruses." But it warns that these methods are not to be confused with "brainwashing, mental torture, or any other form of mental coercion," which are all strictly forbidden.

"These techniques and principles are intended to serve as guides in obtaining the willing cooperation of a source," the manual explains. "The absence of threats in interrogation is intentional, as their enforcement and use normally constitute violations of international law and may result in prosecution under the UCMJ [Uniform Code of Military Justice]."

The Prohibition section ends this way: "[F]rom both legal and moral viewpoints, the restrictions established by international law, agreements, and customs render threats of force, violence, and deprivation useless as interrogation techniques."

Us and Them

Speaking from the Senate floor, McCain explained his reasons for proposing the new law. He drew on his own experience as a POW in the hands of the Viet Cong:

> **Our enemies didn't adhere to the Geneva Conven-tion. Many of my comrades were subjected to very cruel, very inhumane and degrading treatment, a few of them even unto death. But . . . every single one of us knew and took great strength from the belief that we were different from our enemies, that we were better than them, that we, if the roles were reversed, would not disgrace ourselves by committing or countenancing such mistreat-ment of them. That faith was indispensable not only to our survival, but to our attempts to return home with honor. Many of the men I served with would have preferred death to such dishonor.**

He spoke of the new kind of enemy that U.S. soldiers faced in the War on Terrorism: "The enemies we fight today hold such liberal notions in contempt, as they hold the international conventions that enshrine them such as the Geneva Conventions and the treaty on torture in contempt. I know that."

McCain referred to the abuses at Abu Ghraib and other POW prisons and why they had happened. "We de-manded intelligence without ever clearly telling our troops what was permitted and what was forbidden. And then, when things went wrong, we blamed them and we pun-ished them. We have to do better than that."

Yes, he said, intelligence was vital to the War on Ter-rorism, but "the intelligence we collect must be reliable and acquired humanely, under clear standards understood by all our fighting men and women." McCain's bill stated that prisoners must not be coerced or tortured no matter what their nationality or where they were being held.

Finally, he said, "The enemy we fight has no respect for human life or human rights. They don't deserve our sympathy. But this isn't about who they are. This is about who we are. These are the values that distinguish us from our enemies."

Opposing Reactions

Reactions to McCain's proposed law were mixed. The Bush administration strongly opposed it, and some members of Congress sided with the administration. But others

SENATOR JOHN McCAIN, *LEFT*, SHAKES HANDS WITH PRESIDENT GEORGE W. BUSH ON DECEMBER 15, 2005, IN WASHINGTON, D.C. BUSH HAD AGREED TO SIGN THE DETAINEE TREATMENT ACT, WHICH MCCAIN SPONSORED, BANNING CRUEL TREATMENT OF PRISONERS.

did not. Senator Chuck Hagel of Nebraska, himself a former Vietnam POW, said, "I think the administration is making a terrible mistake in opposing John McCain's amendment on detainees and torture. Why in the world they're doing that, I don't know."

The official name for the McCain proposal was the Detainee Treatment Act (DTA). Human rights groups of all kinds lent their support for the DTA. Health care organizations, including the American Psychiatric Association and the American College of Physicians, urged that the amendment become law.

In a letter to U.S. senators, the U.S. Conference of Catholic Bishops wrote:

> **The United States has a long history of leadership and strong support for human rights around the world. . . . We share the concerns of lawmakers and citizens for the safety of U.S. soldiers and civilians abroad in these times of great uncertainty and danger. In the face of this perilous climate, our nation must not embrace a morality based on an attitude that "desperate times call for desperate measures" or "the end justifies the means."**

The DTA Becomes Law— Sort Of

The Detainee Treatment Act, after being adopted by Congress, became law on December 30, 2005. The DTA prohibited the use of torture and other forms of extreme coercion in the interrogation of POWs.

At least it looked that way until President George W. Bush attached a signing statement to the bill. In a signing statement, a president explains how he plans to interpret a new law. Bush wrote that he would interpret the new law "in a manner consistent with the constitutional authority of the president . . . as Commander-in-Chief [and] consistent with the constitutional limitations on the judicial power, which will assist in achieving the shared objective of the Congress and the President . . . of protecting the American people from further terrorist attacks."

Exactly what did these words mean? Here, Bush reserved the right to use his powers as commander in chief to bypass the new DTA law. If he chose, he could allow interrogators to use harsh techniques when questioning prisoners in situations involving national security.

An unnamed administration official speaking to a reporter off the record put it this way: "Of course the president has the obligation to follow this law, [but] he also has the obligation to defend and protect the country as the commander in chief, and he will have to square those two responsibilities in each case."

13

Hamdan v. Rumsfeld

The Bush signing statement was not the only change made to the DTA. An amendment sponsored by U.S. senators Lindsey Graham and Carl Levin was attached, which denied prisoners at Guantanamo Bay Naval Base the right to habeas corpus. The U.S. government could now detain these prisoners in the War on Terrorism forever if it wished, without ever having to bring charges against them.

Contradiction and Confusion

But didn't this amendment violate the U.S. Supreme Court decision in *Rasul* v. *Bush*? That ruling stated that detaining prisoners without charges violated the U.S. Constitution. The Court clearly ruled that the Guantanamo prisoners had the right to habeas corpus. And so *Rasul* v. *Bush* and the Graham-Levin Amendment came to opposite conclusions.

The amendment came with another contradictory pro-

SALIM AHMED HAMDAN, THIRTY-FOUR, WAS CHARGED AS AN AL-QAEDA MEMBER WITH CONSPIRACY TO COMMIT WAR CRIMES. HE WAS AT THE CENTER OF THE *HAMDAN* V. *RUMSFELD* CASE.

vision. The DTA flatly forbade torture and other extreme forms of coercion, yet the Graham-Levin amendment declared that military courts could consider evidence obtained by coercion when putting the Guantanamo prisoners on trial. If evidence obtained by coercion was permitted, then wasn't coercion, including torture, also permitted?

Tom Malinowski, a director at Human Rights Watch, said: "If the McCain law demonstrates to the world that the United States really opposes torture, the Graham-Levin Amendment risks telling the world the opposite."

Sidiki Kaba, president of a French human rights group, said: "This act makes arbitrariness the norm: it codifies lawlessness. The frenzied legislative activity of the Bush administration reinforces our conviction: the unconditional closure of the Guantanamo camp is in the interest of all of humanity."

Guantanamo Under Fire

Ever since its opening in January 2002, the Guantanamo Bay prison had been a flash point of controversy. In 2006, the Associated Press (AP) news organization received previously classified documents concerning Guantanamo prisoners. AP Freedom of Information Act lawsuits forced the Pentagon to declassify and release the documents.

Nearly 8,000 pages were released in all. Most were transcripts of review hearings and Combatant Status Review Tribunals in which prisoners were questioned to see whether they posed a threat to national security.

Since the prison opened, 715 prisoners had been taken in. As of April 2006, 490 remained. The rest were released after U.S. military investigators found them innocent of any wrongdoing. None of those prisoners had been brought to trial.

Some prisoners mentioned in the transcripts had been held at Guantanamo for more than four years. Most said they were innocent and gave assurances that they would remain peaceful if set free. A detainee from Algeria, Mohamed Nechla, was accused of plotting to attack the U.S. embassy in Bosnia. He said, "If I left this place my only concern would be bread on the table for my wife and children."

On the day the documents were released, a Pentagon spokesperson, Bryan Whitman, told reporters about the information Guantanamo interrogators had gained so far. "We've learned about Al-Qaeda's pursuit of WMDs [weapons of mass destruction]. We've learned about their methods of recruitment, location of recruitment centers. We've learned about their skill sets, their terrorist skill sets, both general and specialized operative training."

After examining the declassified documents, the AP found no evidence of any vital information such as Whitman had described. But there could have been evidence at one time. Before release, the transcripts had been edited to delete any passages that might reveal information that could pose a threat to national security.

Dangerous or Innocent?

How many of the remaining prisoners being held at Guantanamo Bay posed a threat to national security? U.S. Senator Dick Durbin of Illinois said:

> **Who are the Guantanamo detainees? Back in 2002, Secretary Rumsfeld described them as "the hardest of the hard core." However, the administration has since released many of them, and it has now become clear that Secretary Rumsfeld's assertion was not completely true. Military**

A Genuine Enemy

One of the prisoners at Guantanamo who showed himself to be a genuine enemy of the United States was Ghassan Abdallah Ghazi al-Shirbi, a Saudi national. He was captured by Pakistani forces in 2002 and handed over to U.S. authorities.

At his military hearing, al-Shirbi was accused of training with Al-Qaeda and of being the right-hand man of Abu Zubaydah, a top Al-Qaeda operative. He also was accused of being trained by Al-Qaeda to operate remote control devices for detonating bombs against U.S. forces in Afghanistan.

Al-Shirbi gladly admitted these and other accusations, and he welcomed the label of enemy combatant. "I came here to tell you I did what I did and I'm willing to pay the price," he said. "Even if I spend hundreds of years in jail, that would be a matter of honor for me."

During his testimony, he lashed out at the United States for its support of Israel and its war with Iraq. "May God help me fight the unfaithful ones," he said.

sources, according to the media, indicate that many detainees have no connection to Al-Qaeda or the Taliban and were sent to Guantanamo over the objections of intelligence personnel who recommended their release.

The United Nations and various human rights groups called for the closing of the Guantanamo Bay prison. Joanne Mariner, an official with Human Rights Watch, said, in May 2006, "Any detainees [at Guantanamo] implicated in criminal acts can and should be charged now. The rest should be released."

President Bush himself joined in the call to close Guantanamo. But, he added, "I also recognize that we're holding some people that are darn dangerous." The decision on whether to close the prison would not be made until after the U.S. Supreme Court handed down its ruling on another case involving the rights of prisoners of war, Bush said.

Prisoners' Legal Rights

That case, known as *Hamdan* v. *Rumsfeld*, concerned the legal rights of Guantanamo prisoners. Detainee Salim Ahmed Hamdan, a citizen of Yemen, had worked as bodyguard and driver for Osama Bin Laden. Hamdan freely admitted his association with Bin Laden but denied any connection with the September 11, 2001, terrorist attacks that Bin Laden's Al-Qaeda terrorist network had carried out. He was charged with conspiracy to commit terrorism and war crimes. If convicted, he could face life in prison.

Ordinarily, suspects such as Hamdan would be tried by military court-martial. But in November 2001, President Bush had issued Military Order No. 1, declaring that foreign terrorist suspects would be tried and sentenced for war crimes by special military commissions with their own unique set of rules and procedures. Hamdan was one of the first Guantanamo detainees chosen to face a military commission trial.

Hamdan's trial began in August 2004. His military attorney, U.S. Navy Lieutenant Commander Charles Swift, immediately challenged the commission's right to try his client. Among the reasons for Swift's challenge were these rules set for military commission trials:

- **A defendant in a commission trial could be barred from being present at his own trial and be convicted on the basis of evidence he would never see.**

- **Evidence obtained by torture could be used against him.**

- **Hearsay evidence also could be used against him. (Hearsay amounts to statements offered by a witness based entirely on what someone else told the witness and that could not be probed by cross-examination or tested for credibility or authenticity.)**

- **A defendant did not have the right to face his accuser and impeach his accuser's testimony.**

- **Even if acquitted by the commission, the defendant could be held as an enemy combatant indefinitely.**

None of these conditions would be legal in criminal trials held in the United States, Swift protested. And none of them was allowed by the Geneva Conventions.

The *Hamdan* Ruling

As a result of Swift's challenge, Hamdan was allowed to file a writ of habeas corpus questioning the military commission's right to try him. The case *Hamdan v. Rumsfeld*, based on Swift's challenge, eventually reached the U.S. Supreme Court.

In June 2006, by a 5-to-3 vote, the High Court ruled in Hamdan's favor. The justices found that the military commissions set up under Military Order No. 1 deprived defendants of basic legal rights and were therefore unconstitutional.

By setting up the commissions without approval of Congress, the president had exceeded his authority as commander in chief, the ruling declared. The commissions were unauthorized, according to both federal and international law and subject to the legal rights granted to prisoners in the 1949 Convention.

War Crimes Worries

The Court's ruling did more than outlaw the administration's military commissions. It also advocated Common Article 3 of the 1949 Convention, which prohibits exposing prisoners to mutilation, torture, violence, and murder, as well as degrading and humiliating treatment. Prisoners in the War on Terrorism must be granted these rights, the Supreme Court ruled, just like POWs in other conflicts.

The administration expressed serious concern about *Hamdan* and the War Crimes Act, the 1996–1997 U.S. statute that criminalized violations of Common Article 3. The statute holds U.S. officials, including the president himself, responsible if detainees should suffer abuse while in U.S. custody, including the death penalty if the crime resulted in death. The administration claimed that Common

Article 3 was not specific enough about how serious the crimes needed to be to warrant prosecution.

Former Army legal expert Lieutenant Colonel Geoffrey S. Corn defended Article 3. It was left deliberately vague, he said, "because efforts to define it would invariably lead to wrongdoers identifying 'exceptions,' and because the meaning was plain—treat people like humans and not animals or objects."

The Unanswered Question

Less than two weeks after the *Hamdan* ruling, the Pentagon announced that it would comply with the High Court's decision. From now on, all detainees in the War on Terrorism would be treated as prisoners of war. Even Al-Qaeda captives would be accorded all the rights spelled out in the 1949 Convention.

But the *Hamdan* ruling left a question of vital importance unanswered. With the administration's military commissions now outlawed, in what sort of court would War on Terrorism prisoners accused of committing war crimes be tried? Common Article 3 of the 1949 Convention states that prisoners shall have "all the judicial guarantees which are recognized as indispensable by civilized peoples." Exactly what were these guarantees that would ensure a fair trial? The Court had deliberately left that question unanswered. It would be up to Congress to decide.

In the aftermath of the *Hamdan* ruling, the administration set to work composing a new set of military commission guidelines to submit for Congress's consideration. Ideally, the administration's new guidelines would maintain a delicate balance between protecting national security and ensuring that terrorist suspects received a fair trial.

14

The Military Commissions Act

Lawmakers in the House and Senate discussed, debated, and modified the Republican administration's guidelines for a new kind of military court for trying War on Terrorism suspects. The result was the Military Commissions Act (MCA), passed in October 2006 despite the objections of many Democrats and some Republicans. A Democrat who opposed the act, Senator Patrick Leahy of Vermont, called it a "total rollback of everything this country has stood for."

The MCA and Torture

This "rollback" included the issue of using torture when interrogating prisoners. According to President Bush, the act officially bans the use of torture. But the act also leaves it up to the president to decide what interrogation techniques are allowed, while allowing him to keep those authorized techniques secret from the public. Bush said, "[T]he reason we don't talk about [interrogation] techniques is because we don't want the enemy to be able to adjust. We're in a war."

THIS ARTIST'S SKETCH DEPICTS THE SCENE AT A PRELIMINARY HEARING AT THE U.S. NAVAL BASE AT GUANTANAMO BAY, CUBA, ON AUGUST 24, 2004. DEFENDANT SALIM AHMED HAMDAN (*SECOND FROM LEFT*) AND HIS LAWYER, LIEUTENANT COMMANDER CHARLES SWIFT (*THIRD FROM LEFT*) ARE FACING A PANEL OF U.S. MILITARY OFFICERS.

The MCA also permits the CIA interrogation program, along with its use of aggressive interrogation techniques, such as stripping prisoners and exposing them to extremely cold temperatures and sleep deprivation, to continue. Bush called the CIA program in which prisoners are interrogated in secret locations a "vital tool to protect the American people for years to come" and "one of the most successful intelligence efforts in American history."

Senator John McCain was one of the Republicans who voted in favor of the new law. He said that in passing the Military Commissions Act, "[t]here's no doubt that the integrity and letter and spirit of the Geneva Conventions have been preserved."

Opposing legislators expressed dismay at what they saw as McCain's flip-flop from his previous vehement opposition to the use of torture on prisoners. Apparently, McCain had given in to the president on the torture issue. Speaking from the floor of the U.S. Senate, Democratic Senator John Kerry of Massachusetts said: "Let me be clear about something—something that it seems few people are willing to say. This bill permits torture. . . . This bill gives an administration that lobbied for torture exactly what it wanted."

Kerry went on to say:

So, what are we voting for with this bill? We are voting to give the President the power to interpret the Geneva Conventions. . . . The only guarantee we have that these provisions really will prohibit torture is the word of the President. . . . But the word of the President today is questioned. This administration said there were weapons of mass destruction in Iraq, that Saddam Hussein had ties to Al-Qaeda, that they would exhaust diplomacy before we went to war, that the insurgency was in its last throes. None of these statements were true, and now we find our troops in the crossfire of civil war in Iraq with no end in sight. They keep saying the war in Iraq is making us safer, but our own intelligence agencies say it is actually fanning the flames of jihad, creating a whole new generation of terrorists and putting our country at greater risk of terrorist attack. It is no wonder then that we are hesitant to blindly accept the word of the President on this question today.

President Bush saw things differently. In a TV interview about the MCA, he said that he wanted to "assure the American people that we were within the law and we don't torture—I've said all along to the American people: we won't torture. But we need to be in a position where we can interrogate these people."

Bush also said:

> **With this bill America reaffirms our determination to win the War on Terror. The passage of time will not dull our memory or sap our nerve. We will fight this war with confidence and with clear purpose. We will protect our country and our people. We will work with our friends and allies across the world to defend our way of life. We will leave behind a freer, safer and more peaceful world for those who follow us.**

The MCA and Legal Rights

President Bush also said of the MCA, "With our actions, we will send a clear message to those who kill Americans: We will find you and we will bring you to justice." But critics objected strongly to the unprecedented powers the MCA gave the president in regard to holding and prosecuting prisoners of war. Anthony D. Romero is executive director of the American Civil Liberties Union (ACLU), a national organization dedicated to defending people's constitutional rights. Romero called the MCA "unconstitutional and un-American." He said:

> **Nothing separates America more from our enemies than our commitment to fairness and the rule of law, but the bill signed today is an historic break because it turns Guantanamo Bay and other U.S. facilities into legal no-man's-lands. . . . Nothing could be further from the American values we all hold in our hearts than the Military Commissions Act.**

Romero was referring to MCA provisions that governed the trials of War on Terrorism suspects accused of committing war crimes, including the admission of hearsay evidence and evidence obtained by coercion. Hearsay evidence and coerced evidence are seldom admitted in civil or military trials.

Romero also was referring to other MCA provisions that govern a suspect's legal rights. Chief among these are passages in the act that suspend the fundamental principle of habeas corpus. Suspects may be held indefinitely without a trial, with no legal right to challenge their detention in a court of law, and no knowledge of the charges against them. Yet Article I, Section IX of the U.S. Constitution states that habeas corpus may be suspended only "in cases of rebellion or invasion." In addition, the U.S. Supreme Court, in its *Rasul* v. *Bush* ruling, had forbidden the administration from suspending prisoners' rights of habeas corpus. The MCA appeared to be ignoring these fundamental prohibitions against suspending habeas corpus.

The MCA also gave President Bush the power to detain people who never set foot on a battlefield and had never been involved in any hostile acts toward the United States. Any foreigner whom Bush chose to label an "illegal enemy combatant" might be held forever. This included noncitizens living legally and permanently within the United States (green-card holders) and foreign citizens living in their own countries.

The MCA and Immunity from Prosecution

Various human rights groups and journalists had investigated and documented hundreds of cases of detainee abuse in the War on Terrorism involving behavior that could be seen as inhumane. Cases reportedly included instances

The Passaro Case

The MCA did not protect U.S. government employees from offenses involving torture or murder. According to the Army's Mikolashek Report, at least twenty detainees had died in sixteen prisons in Iraq and Afghanistan since the War on Terrorism began.

As of November 2006, only one person had been indicted in federal court for any of these deaths. That was CIA contractor David Passaro, who was tried for beating a civilian Afghan detainee to death in 2003. The victim, Abdul Wali, a farmer, was being questioned about rocket attacks on a U.S. base. Wali insisted he was not involved in the attacks.

A federal jury in a North Carolina court found Passaro guilty. CIA Director Michael Hayden reacted to the verdict by sending this message to his employees: "Passaro's actions were unlawful, reprehensible and neither authorized nor condoned by the Agency. It is important for all of us to remember that his actions were totally inconsistent with the normal conduct of CIA officers and contractors, who reflect the core values of our nation."

where the abuse was committed with the approval of higher-ups in the military chain of command and even civilian officials. Could government employees, even high-ranking officials, be tried for these abuses?

The Bush administration had provisions included in the MCA to address these concerns. The act protects CIA and military personnel from all but the severest abuses involving torture and murder.

It also immunizes members of the Bush administration from prosecution for violations of the U.S. War Crimes Act committed in the past. They would be exempted from domestic war crimes prosecutions for offenses committed at Abu Ghraib, Guantanamo, and other U.S.-run prisons that involved humiliating and degrading prisoners, such as forcing them to stand naked or to crawl while attached to a dog leash.

These MCA provisions governing torture, legal rights, and immunity from prosecution were highly controversial. They would soon be challenged.

15
The Debate Continues

In November 2006, two separate legal challenges were made to the conduct of the Bush administration in regard to the treatment of prisoners of war. One involved U.S. law, the other international law.

A U.S. Challenge

Janet Reno served as U.S. attorney general from 1993 to 2001 in the administration of Democratic President Bill Clinton. Until the MCA was passed, she had not spoken out about the Bush administration's policies on prisoners of war. In November 2006, Reno, along with seven other former Justice Department prosecutors, filed court papers citing the dangers of trying suspects outside of the traditional court system.

Their challenge was based on a case involving Ali Saleh Kahlah al-Marri, the only War on Terrorism detainee to be held on United States soil. The suspected Al-Qaeda agent was arrested in the United States in 2001, declared an enemy combatant, and imprisoned at a naval base in South Carolina.

The court papers challenged the Justice Department's right to try al-Marri because, according to the MCA, he would have no right to challenge his imprisonment in U.S. civilian courts. Justice Department spokesperson Kathleen Blomquist stated the Bush administration's position: "These are complex and difficult legal issues, and while we respect the right of other legal minds to be heard on these issues, we believe we are on firm legal footing in this case." As of January 2007, the Fourth U.S. Circuit Court of Appeals in Richmond, Virginia, was considering the case.

An International Challenge

Defense Secretary Donald Rumsfeld, U.S. Attorney General Alberto Gonzales, and other top U.S. officials took no responsibility for the humiliation and torture documented at the Abu Ghraib and Guantanamo Bay prison camps. They contended that the Abu Ghraib crimes had been strictly the work of a few low-ranking soldiers who briefly went out of control, and that nothing in the way of torture ever occurred at Guantanamo Bay prison.

That's why a coalition of human rights groups—the Center for Constitutional Rights (CCR), based in New York, along with the Republican Lawyer's Association of Berlin, Germany—took action. In November 2006, they filed a complaint with the German courts on behalf of five Iraqi citizens mistreated by U.S. soldiers at Baghdad's Abu Ghraib prison. The alleged mistreatment included electric shock treatment, severe beatings, sleep and food deprivation, and sexual abuse.

The coalition chose the German courts because Germany's Code of Crimes Against International Law grants these courts the duty to prosecute war crimes committed anywhere in the world when sufficient evidence exists. CCR vice president Peter Weiss said that the coalition took action because "the U.S. government [was] not willing to open an investigation into allegations against these officials."

By "these officials," Weiss meant Rumsfeld, Gonzales, former CIA director George Tenet, Under Secretary of Defense for Intelligence Steven Cambone, Lieutenant General Ricardo Sanchez, former Brigadier General Janis Karpinski, and other military officers who served in Iraq. The MCA made these officials immune from federal prosecution in the United States but did not immunize them against international war crimes prosecution. The case was turned over to Germany's federal prosecutor, who would decide whether the case merited further investigation.

Reasons for Humane Treatment

The challenges issued by the eight former federal prosecutors and by the coalition of human rights groups seem shocking in light of America's practice of humane treatment of POWs, a longstanding tradition beginning with George Washington's order in the year 1776 to "treat them with humanity." While British forces insisted on executing Colonial captives outright, Washington ordered that captives on the British side be treated humanely.

With that historic order, Washington resisted the powerful temptations present in any war when soldiers are taken prisoner. What's to stop the captors from abusing members of the hated enemy forces subdued and at their mercy?

Ethics and morals, such as the Golden Rule, play a part. As Washington said, it was the right thing to do. Pride and honor are also factors. U.S. soldiers can take great strength from the belief that they are better than their enemies. Positive reciprocity figures in as well. As General Dwight D. Eisenhower said, he did not want to give Hitler an excuse for treating U.S. prisoners more harshly than the Nazis already were treating them. Finally, there are the Geneva Conventions and other documents of

From Dictator to Prisoner of War

Even national leaders can become prisoners of war. On December 13, 2003, U.S. forces in the Iraq War captured Iraqi dictator Saddam Hussein in a village in the town of Al-Dawr, near his birthplace in Awja. Iraqi citizens were shocked to see the man who had ruled them with such an iron fist for more than three decades filthy and crouching in a hole in the ground, now a prisoner of war.

On October 19, 2005, Hussein was put on trial in a Baghdad, Iraq, courtroom for crimes against humanity. Among his crimes were the jailing, torture, and executions of 148 Shi'ite villagers in the town of Dujail in 1982. Many more were sent to a remote desert prison. All the homes and palm groves in Dujail were demolished.

On November 5, 2006, Hussein was sentenced to death by hanging for his crimes against the Shi'ite villagers. Iraq's former leader remained defiant to the end. As the judge read the guilty verdict, he cried out to the court: "You don't issue sentences; you are servants of those who want to colonize us," meaning the U.S. forces who were occupying Iraq. On December 30, 2006, in Baghdad, Hussein was executed.

international humanitarian law that hold the signing nations to a promise that they will treat POWs humanely.

Reasons for Inhumane Treatment

Despite these humanitarian incentives, prisoners of war have been and continue to be mistreated. No nation can claim a perfect record. Reasons have been many and varied.

During the American Revolutionary War, the British executed colonial captives. They saw them as murderous rebels and not legitimate soldiers fighting under the laws and customs of war.

During many wars, such as the American Civil War and World War I, shortages of funds and other realities of war kept getting in the way. It was often difficult, if not impossible, to supply prisoners with enough nutritious food and warm clothing and shelter to keep them healthy. It also put a strain on the captor army to devote soldiers and medical personnel to guarding and caring for captives.

In World War II, the Soviets mistreated German prisoners because the Germans mistreated Soviet prisoners. During the Korean and Vietnam wars, U.S. prisoners were brainwashed, tortured, and publicly humiliated for propaganda purposes.

In the War on Terrorism, U.S. government personnel used aggressive methods to interrogate prisoners. While in violation of both national and international laws, these abusive tactics were said by Bush administration officials to be necessary to save American lives.

Both history and present trends suggest that prisoners of war will continue to test the limits of human behavior. The treatment of POWs indicates that war is not just an outward conflict of nations and ideologies. War is also an interior struggle between the humane and the inhumane sides of human nature.

Notes

Introduction
p. 7, par. 4, "McCain, John Sydney III," The P.O.W. Network, http://www.pownetwork.org/bios/m/m125.htm

Chapter One
p. 12, pars. 2–3,"Protecting POW'S," *Online NewsHour*, March 24, 2003, http://www.pbs.org/newshour/bb/middle_east/jan june03/pow_3-24.html

Chapter Two
p. 15, par. 1, "War Quotes," The Quotations Page, http://www.quotationspage.com/quotes/Georges_Clemenceau/

p. 15, par. 1, "War Quotes," The Quotations Page, http://www.quotationspage.com/quote/11252.html

pp. 16–17, Ernie Pyle, "The God-Damned Infantry," May 2, 1943, http://www.journalism.indiana.edu/news/erniepyle/goddamninfantry.html

p. 18, par. 5, William James Stover, *Preemptive War: The Legal and Moral Implications of the Bush and Rumsfeld Doctrines* (Ignatian Center, Banner Institute, Santa Clara University, Santa Clara, CA, 2003), http://www.scu.edu/ignatiancenter/bannan/publications/explore/fall03/pre emtivewar.cfm

p. 19, par. 1, Jean-Jacques Rousseau, quoted in "International Humanitarian Law," p. 7. ICRC, http://www.icrc.org/Web/Eng/siteeng0.nsf/htmlall/p0703/$File/ICRC_002_0703.PDF!Open

p. 19, par. 4, Alex Markels, quoted in "Will Terrorism Rewrite the Laws of War?" *NPR*, December 6, 2005, http://www.

npr.org/templates/story/story.php?storyId=5011464

p. 21, par. 2, "Andersonville: Prisoner of War Camp," About. com, http://militaryhistory.about.com/gi/dynamic/offsite. htm?zi=1/XJ&sdn=militaryhistory&zu=http%3A%2F%2 Fwww.cr.nps.gov%2Fnr%2Ftwhp%2Fwwwlps%2Flesson s%2F11andersonville%2F11andersonville.htm

p. 22, par. 3, John McElroy, *This Was Andersonville*, Ray Meredith, ed. (New York: Fairfax Press, 1979), 79.

p. 24, par. 3, Francis Lieber, "The Lieber Code of 1863," April 24, 1863, http://www.civilwarhome.com/liebercode.htm

Chapter Three

p. 27, par. 1, Henri Dunant, *A Memory of Solferino*, 1862, quoted in "From the battle of Solferino to the eve of the First World War," ICRC, December 28, 2004, http://www.icrc.org/web/eng/siteeng0.nsf/html/57JNVP

p. 28, par. 2–3, "Convention for the Amelioration of the Condition of the Wounded in Armies in the Field," Geneva, Switzerland, August 22, 1864, http://www.yale.edu/law web/avalon/lawofwar/geneva04.htm#art1

p. 29, par. 1–4, "Laws of War: Laws and Customs of War on Land (Hague IV)," The Hague, The Netherlands, October 18, 1907, http://www.yale.edu/lawweb/avalon/lawofwar /hague04.htm#iart1

Chapter Four

p. 30, par. 1, "Casualties First World War," Spartacus Educational, http://www.spartacus.schoolnet.co.uk/FWWdeaths. htm

p. 30, par. 1, "Prisoners of War," The Museum of the Great War, 2001, http://www.historial.org/us/objet/prison.htm

p. 33, pars. 2–6, "Convention of July 27, 1929, Relative to the Treatment of Prisoners of War," Geneva, Switzerland, July 27, 1929, http://www.yale.edu/lawweb/avalon/lawofwar/ geneva02.htm

p. 33, par. 7, p. 36, pars. 2–5, "Laws of War: Laws and Customs of War on Land (Hague IV)," The Hague, The Netherlands, October 18, 1907.

pp. 34–35, Reginald Morris, "Memoirs and Diaries: First Days of Imprisonment," First World War.com, November 25, 2001, http://www.firstworldwar.com/diaries/firstdaysof imprisonment.htm

Chapter Five

p. 37, par. 3–p. 38, par. 1, Dwight D. Eisenhower, *Crusade in Europe*, (New York: Doubleday, 1948), 469.

p. 38, par. 3, Ontario Consultants on Religious Tolerance. "Shared Belief in the Golden Rule," ReligiousTolerance. org, http://www.religioustolerance.org/reciproc.htm

p. 39, par. 2, Arnold Krammer, *Nazi Prisoners of War in America*, (New York: Scarborough House, 1992), 256.

p. 43, pars. 4–5, Quoted in Jack Hamann, *On American Soil* (Chapel Hill, North Carolina: Algonquin Books), 2005, http://www.npr.org/templates/story/story.php?storyId=4659346

p. 45, par. 3, Quoted in John W. Dower, *Embracing Defeat: Japan in the Wake of World War II*, (New York: Norton, 2000), 516.

p. 46, Gavan Daws, *Prisoners of the Japanese: POWs of World War II in the Pacific*, (New York: Quill, William Morrow, 1994), 336.

p. 48, par. 2, "Nuremberg War Crimes Trial," Spartacus Educational, http://www.spartacus.schoolnet.co.uk/2WWnuremberg.htm

Chapter Six

p. 50, par. 3–p. 51, par. 1, "The Atlantic Conference: Joint Statement by President Roosevelt and Prime Minister Churchill, August 14, 1941," http://www.yale.edu/lawweb/avalon/wwii/atlantic/at10.htm

p. 52, par. 2–p. 53, par. 1, "Universal Declaration of Human Rights," United Nations Office of the High Commissioner for Human Rights," December 10, 1948, http://www.unhchr.ch/udhr/lang/eng.htm

pp. 54–56, "Convention (III) relative to the Treatment of Prisoners of War. Geneva, 12 August 1949," ICRC, http://www.icrc.org/ihl.nsf/7c4d08d9b287a42141256739003e636b/6fef854a3517b75ac125641e004a9e68

p. 57, par. 1, "The Paris Treaty (Peace Treaty of 1783)," Early America.com, http://www.earlyamerica.com/earlyamerica/milestones/paris/text.html

p. 58, par. 3, "Convention of July 27, 1929."

p. 58, par. 3, "Convention (III)."

Chapter Seven

p. 62, par. 6, Michael Hedges, "For POWs Korea Was Not 'America's Forgotten War,'" Scripps Howard News Service, November 11, 1999, http://www.rt66.com/~korteng/SmallArms/Not_Forgotten_By_Some.htm

p. 64, par. 1, Hedges.

p. 65, par. 2, Julia Layton, "How Brainwashing Works," How StuffWorks, http://people.howstuffworks.com/brainwashing1.htm

Chapter Eight

p. 67, par. 5, "Vietnam's Hanoi Hilton: Hell on Earth," The Vietnam War, http://www.vietnamwar.com/hanoihilton.htm.

p. 68, John G. Hubbell, *P.O.W.: A Definitive History of the American Prisoner-of-War Experience in Vietnam, 1964–1973* (Lincoln, NE: iUniverse.Com, Inc., 2000), 10–18.

p. 71, par. 1, Hubbell, 193.

p. 71, par. 5, Hubbell, 198.

p. 72, par. 4,–p. 73, p. 3, Don Luce, "The Tiger Cages of Viet Nam," Historians Against the War, http://www.historiansagainst war.org/resources/torture/luce.html

p. 73, par. 2, William H. Forman Jr., "The U.S. POW Experience Since World War II, http://www.isanet.org/noarchive/forman.htm

p. 75, par. 4, "Testimony of Dr. Stephen J. Morris–July 14, 1993," Foreign Relations Subcommittee for Asian and Pacific Affairs, July 14, 1993, http://www.aiipowmia.com/testimony/morristst.html

Chapter Nine

p. 80, par. 1, "In Search of Al Qaeda," *Frontline*: Teacher Center, http://www.pbs.org/wgbh/pages/frontline/teach/alqaeda/glossary.html

p. 83, par. 3, p. 84, pars. 1–2, p. 85, par. 3, "Convention (III)."

p. 87, par. 1, Donald Rumsfeld, "Memorandum to the Joint Chiefs of Staff," January 19, 2002, http://www.lawofwar.org/Rums feld%20Torture%20memo_0001.jpg.

p. 87, par. 3, Rumsfeld.

p. 87, par. 4, "The Rumsfeld Order January 19, 2002", International Law of War Association, http://www.lawofwar.org/Torture_Memos_analysis.htm

p. 87, par. 5–p. 88, par. 1, Alberto R. Gonzales, "Memorandum for the President," January 25, 2002, http://www.msnbc.com/modules/newsweek/pdf/gonzales_memo.pdf

p. 88, par. 2, "Convention (III)."

p. 88, par. 3, Jane Mayer, "The Hidden Power," *The New Yorker*, July 6, 2003, www.newyorker.com/fact/content/articles/060703fa_fact1

p. 90, par. 4, Gonzales.

p. 91, par. 4, Colin L. Powell, "Draft Decision Memorandum for the President on the Applicability of the Geneva Convention to the Conflict in Afghanistan," January 26, 2002, http://www.msnbc.msn.com/id/4999363/site/newsweek/

p. 92, pars. 1–3, Richard Waddington, "Guantanamo Inmates Are POWs Despite Bush View—ICRC," Common Dreams News Center, February 8, 2002, http://www.commondreams.org/cgi-bin/print.cgi?file=/headlines02/0208–04.htm

p. 93, pars. 1–3, "Body of Principles for the Protection of All Persons under Any Form of Detention or Imprisonment," United Nations Office of the High Commissioner for Human Rights, December 9, 1988, http://www.unhchr.ch/html/menu3/b/h_comp36.htm

Chapter Ten
p. 94, par. 1, "Our Mission," Center for Constitutional Rights, http://www.ccrny.org/v2/home.asp

p. 95, par. 2, "Convention (III)."

pp. 96–97, "International Covenant on Civil and Political Rights," United Nations, December 16, 1966, http://www.unhchr.ch/html/menu3/b/a_ccpr.htm

p. 98, par. 1, ICRC, "Commentary: IV Geneva Convention Relative to the Protection of Civilian Persons in Time of War, Geneva, 1958," quoted in " *Time* Falsely Claimed that Geneva Conventions Protect Only POWs," Media Matters, http://www.mediamatters.org/items/200506060005

p. 98, par. 3, Quoted in "Remarks of the Right Honourable Beverley McLachlin, P.C. to the Vietnam-Canadian Business Association," Supreme Court of Canada, November

28, 2003, www.scc-csc.gc.ca/aboutcourt/judges/speeches/ Vietnam_e.asp

p. 100, par. 3, *Rasul et al. v. Bush, President of the United States, et al.*, June 28, 2004, Supreme Court of the United States, http://www.law.cornell.edu/supct/html/03–334.ZS. html

Chapter Eleven

p. 102, par. 1, "Convention Against Torture and Other Cruel, Inhuman or Degrading Treatment or Punishment," United Nations Office of the High Commissioner for Human Rights, December 10, 1984, http://www.unhchr.ch/html /menu3/b/h_cat39.htm

p. 103, par. 1, "A Summary of United Nations Agreements on Human Rights: Convention Against Torture." http://www. hrweb.org/legal/undocs.html#CAT

p. 103, par. 2, "Convention (III)."

p. 103, par. 3, Dana Priest, and R. Jeffrey Smith, "Memo Offered Justification for Use of Torture," *The Washington Post*, June 8, 2004, A01.

p. 103, par. 4, Gonzales.

p. 104, par. 1, "Convention Against Torture."

p. 104, par. 2, Quoted in Peter Brooks, "The Plain Meaning of Torture," *Slate*, February 9, 2005, http://www.slate.com/ id/2113314

p. 104, par. 3, Dana Priest, and R. Jeffrey Smith, "Memo Offered Justification for Use of Torture," *The Washington Post*, June 8, 2004, A01.

p. 104, par. 4, Dana Priest, and Joe Stephens, "Secret World of U.S. Interrogation," *The Washington Post*, May 11, 2004, AO1.

p. 105, Dick Durbin, "U.S. Senate Floor Statement by Sen. Dick Durbin on Guantanamo Bay," June 14, 2005, http:// durbin.senate.gov/gitmo.cfm

p. 107, par. 2, Jane Mayer, "A Deadly Interrogation," *The New Yorker*, July 11, 2005, http://www.newyorker.com/ fact/content/articles/051114fa_fact

p. 107, par. 2, "Abu Ghraib Abuse Photos," Antiwar.com, http://www.antiwar.com/news/?articleid=8560

p. 107, par. 3, "Beyond Abu Ghraib: Detention and Torture in Iraq." May 2004. Amnesty International. http://web. amnesty.org/library/Index/ENGMDE140012006

p. 107, par. 4, Anthony Taguba, "Article 15–6 Investigation of the 800th Military Police Brigade," http://news.findlaw.com/cnn/docs/iraq/tagubarpt.html#ThR1.9

p. 108, par. 2, Josh White, and Scott Higham, "Abuses an aberration, report says 94 cases confirmed or called possible—individuals blamed," *San Francisco Chronicle*, July 23, 2004. http://www.sfgate.com/cgi-bin/article.cgi?file=/c/a/2004/07/23/MNGQH7RTQ21.DTL

p. 108, par. 5, Priest and Stephens.

p. 109, par. 2, "UN Body Criticizes US on Rights," *BBC News*, July 26, 2006, http://news.bbc.co.uk/go/pr/fr//2/hi/americas/5223586.stm

p. 109, par. 3, Priest and Stephens.

p. 111, par. 4, Dana Priest, "CIA Holds Terror Suspects in Secret Prisons," *The Washington Post*, November 2, 2005, A01.

p. 111, par. 4, Brian Ross, and Richard Esposito, "CIA's Harsh Interrogation Techniques Described," *ABC News*, November 19, 2005, http://www.commondreams.org/headlines05/111905.htm

p. 112, par. 5–p. 113, par. 1, Dana Priest and Joe Stephens.

p. 112, par. 5–p. 113, par. 1, Doug Struck, "Canadian Was Falsely Accused, Panel Says," *Washington Post*. September 19, 2006, A01.

p. 113, pars. 2–5, Brian Ross.

p. 113, par. 4, Jane Mayer, "Outsourcing Torture," *The New Yorker*, February 14, 2005, http://www.newyorker.com/printables/fact/050214fa_fact6

p. 114, par. 2, George W. Bush, "Statement by the President: United Nations International Day in Support of Victims of Torture," The White House, Washington, D.C., June 26, 2003, http://www.whitehouse.gov/news/releases/2003/06/20030626-3.html

p. 114, par. 3, Quoted in James G. Lakely, "'Values' Guided Bush Torture Ban," *Washington Times*, June 23, 2004, www.washingtontimes.com/national/20040623-124644-1098r.htm

p. 114, par. 4, Jane Mayer, "Outsourcing Torture."

Chapter Twelve

p. 116, *FM 34–52*, Headquarters, Department of the Army, Washington, DC, May 8, 1987, Chapter 1, Interrogation and the Interrogator, http://www.globalsecurity.org/intell/

library/policy/army/fm/fm34-52/chapter1.htm

p. 117, pars. 1–2, John McCain, "Detainee Amendment Closing Statement," October 5, 2005, http://mccain.senate.gov/index.cfm?fuseaction=Newscenter.ViewPressRelease&Content_id=1701

p. 117, par. 3–p. 118, par. 2, John McCain, "McCain Statement on Detainee Amendments," October 5, 2005, http://mccain.senate.gov/index.cfm?fuseaction=NewsCenter.ViewPressRelease&Content_id=1611

p. 119, par. 1, Quoted in "Hagel: Torture Exemption Would Be Mistake," Associated Press, November 6, 2005, http://www.nytimes.com/aponline/national/AP-Congress-Detainees.html

p. 119, par. 3, Quoted in "USCCB supports McCain amendment on treatment of 'enemy combatants,'" *Salt of the Earth*, October 4, 2005, http://salt.claretianpubs.org/washweek/2005/10/is0510a.html

p. 120, par. 1, "Amnesty International's Supplementary Briefing to the UN Committee Against Torture," Amnesty International, May 3, 2006, http://web.amnesty.org/library/index/engamr510612006

p. 120, par. 3, Charlie Savage, "Bush could bypass new torture ban," *Boston Globe*, January 4, 2006, http://www.boston.com/news/nation/articles/2006/01/04/bush_could_bypass_new_torture_ban?m

Chapter Thirteen

p. 123, par. 2, "Landmark Torture Ban Undercut," Human Rights Watch, December 16, 2005, http://hrw.org/english/docs/2005/12/16/usdom12311.htm

p. 123, par. 3, "The 'Detainee Treatment Act,' strips Federal Courts of jurisdiction over the fate of detainees at Guantánamo," FIDH, January 24, 2006, http://www.fidh.org/article_print.php3?id_article=3004

p. 124, par 2, Andrew Selsky, "Pentagon releases new Guantanamo Bay transcripts, shedding light on detainees," *Associated Press*, April 3, 2006, http://www.ap.org/pages/about/whatsnew/wn_040506a.html

p. 125, "Ghassan Abdallah Ghazi Al Shirbi," Answers.com, www.answers.com/topic/ghassan-abdallah-ghazi-al-shirbi

p. 125, Tim Golden, "Voices Baffled, Brash and Irate in Guantanamo," *New York Times*, March 6, 2006, http://www.

nytimes.com/learning/students/pop/articles/06gitmo.html

p. 126, par. 4, p. 126, par. 1, Durbin.

p. 126, par. 2, "Bush Should Close Guantanamo Now," Human Rights Watch, May 9, 2006, http:www.//hrw.org/english/docs/2006/05/09/usdom13332.htm

p. 126, par. 3, "Supreme Court Blocks Trials at Guantanamo," *Associated Press*, June 29, 2006, www.nytimes.com/2006/06/29/washington/29cndscotus.html?hp&ex=1151640000&en=1aa0983620edfa9b&ei=5094&partner=homepage

p. 129, par. 2, Jeffrey R. Smith, "War Crimes Act Changes Would Reduce Threat of Prosecution," *Washington Post*, August 9, 2006, A01.

Chapter Fourteen

p. 131, par. 1, Greg Kelly, "Bush Signs Law for Tough Interrogation of Terror Suspects," Fox News, October 17, 2006, http://www.foxnews.com/story/0,2933,221480,00.html

p. 131, par. 2, "The Abuse Can Continue," *The Washington Post*, September 22, 2006, A16

p. 132, par. 2, "Congressional Record: Military Commissions Act of 2006, the United States Senate," GovTrack.US. September 28, 2006, http://www.govtrack.us/congress/record.xpd?id=109–s20060928–14&person=300092

p. 133, pars. 1–3, Kelly.

p. 135, par. 2, John Sifton, "Criminal, Immunize Thyself," *Slate*, August 11, 2006, http://www.slate.com/id/2147585/

p. 135, par. 3, "Passaro's Judgment Day," *News & Observer*, Raleigh, North Carolina, August 20, 2006, http://www.newsobserver.com/579/story/476976.html

Chapter Fifteen

p. 138, par. 1, Matt Apuzzo, "Reno Files Challenge to Terror Law," *Associated Press*, November 20, 2006, http://www.washingtonpost.com/wp-dyn/content/article/2006/11/20/AR2006112000957_pf.html

p. 139, par. 1, "Rumsfeld Sued for Alleged War Crimes," *Deutsche Welle*, November 28, 2006, http://www.dw-world.de/dw/article/0,1564,1413907,00.html

p. 141, Nancy A. Youssef, "Amid Joy, Iraqis Gird for Tumult," *Kansas City Star*, November 6, 2006, http://www.kansascity.com/mld/kansascity/15939362.htm

All Internet sites were accurate and available when sent to press.

Further Information

Further Reading

Banfield, Susan. *The Andersonville Prison War Crimes Trial*. Berkeley Heights, NJ: Enslow, 2000.

Feinberg, Barbara Jane. *John McCain*. Brookfield, CT: Millbrook, 2000.

Martin, M. *The Iraqi Prison Abuse Scandal*. San Diego, CA: Lucent Books, 2005.

Myers, Walter Dean. *A Place Called Heartbreak: a Story of Vietnam*. Woodridge, IL: Sagebrush, 2001.

Stein, R. Conrad. *Prisoners of War*. Riverside, CT: Children's Press, 1987.

Web Sites

These Web sites are good places to pick up information and ideas on the people, places, events, and ideas discussed in this book.

First World War.Com: Vintage Photographs of War
http://www.firstworldwar.com/photos/prisoners.htm
Hundreds of photographs of World War I, including photos of life in POW camps, with explanatory text. Clicking on any of the thumbnail photos gives a full-screen version.

Geneva Conventions
http://www.icrc.org/Web/Eng/siteeng0.nsf/html/genevaconven tions
This site, created by the International Committee of the Red Cross, gives the full text of each of the four major Geneva Conventions, including number three on prisoners of war. It also gives concise descriptions of different aspects of international humanitarian law.

How the Rules of War Work
http://people.howstuffworks.com/rules-of-war.htm
A concise, straightforward series of explanations about the rules of war, including a section on prisoners of war.

International Human Rights Instruments
http://www.unhchr.ch/html/intlinst.htm
The United Nations maintains this site, a list of links to the texts of dozens of major human rights documents relating to the treatment of prisoners of war as well as other human rights issues.

OnWar.com
http://www.onwar.com/
This Web site documents over 1,500 armed conflicts from the years 1800 to 1999. Included are major and minor interstate wars, extra-state warfare, rebellions and revolutions around the globe.

POW Stories
http://www.pegasusarchive.org/pow/
Ex-POWs from World War II tell their true stories of survival.

Bibliography

Carlson, Lewis H. *Remembered Prisoners of a Forgotten War: An Oral History of Korean War POWs*. New York: St. Martins Griffin, 2003.

Daws, Gavan. *Prisoners of the Japanese: POWs of World War II in the Pacific*. New York: Quill, William Morrow, 1994.

Hubbell, John G. *P.O.W.: A Definitive History of the American Prisoner-of-War Experience in Vietnam, 1964–1973*. Lincoln, NE: iUniverse.Com, Inc., 2000.

Lewis, George G., and John Mewha. *History of Prisoner of War Utilization by the United States Army 1776–1945*. Honolulu, HI: University Press of the Pacific, 2002.

McCain, John, and John Salter. *Faith of My Fathers: A Family Memoir*. New York: Harper Paperbacks, 2000.

Rochester, Stewart I., and Frederick T. Kiley. *Honor Bound: The History of American Prisoners of War in Southeast Asia, 1961–1973*. Honolulu, HI: University Press of the Pacific, 2005.

Index

Page numbers in **boldface** are illustrations, tables, and charts.

154

About the Author

Ron Fridell has written for radio, TV, newspapers, and textbooks. He has written books on social and political issues, such as terrorism and espionage, and scientific topics, such as DNA fingerprinting and global warming. His most recent book for Marshall Cavendish Benchmark was *Environmental Issues* in this series. He taught English as a second language while a member of the Peace Corps in Bangkok, Thailand. He lives in Tucson, Arizona, with his wife Patricia and his dog, an Australian Shepherd named Madeline.